Village '
in
DEVON

Michael Bennie

COUNTRYSIDE BOOKS
NEWBURY BERKSHIRE

First published 1998
© Michael Bennie 1998

COUNTRYSIDE BOOKS
3 Catherine Road
Newbury, Berkshire

ISBN 1 85306 504 8

Designed by Graham Whiteman
Photographs by the author
Maps by Jonathan Bennie
Illustrations by Trevor Yorke

Produced through MRM Associates Ltd., Reading
Printed by Woolnough Bookbinding Ltd., Irthlingborough

Contents

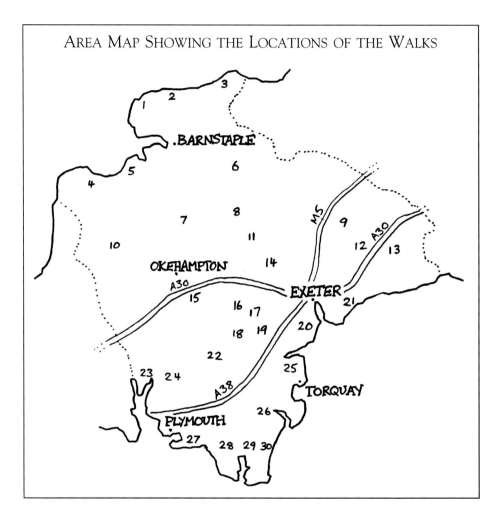

AREA MAP SHOWING THE LOCATIONS OF THE WALKS

Publisher's Note

We hope that you obtain considerable enjoyment from this book; great care has been taken in its preparation. Although at the time of publication all routes followed public rights of way or permitted paths, diversion orders can be made and permissions withdrawn.

   We cannot of course be held responsible for such diversion orders and any inaccuracies in the text which result from these or any other changes to the routes, nor any damage which might result from walkers trespassing on private property. We are anxious though that all details covering the walks are kept up to date and would therefore welcome information from readers which would be relevant to future editions.

WALK

Introduction

For me, one of Devon's main attractions is the variety of its landscape. From its rugged coasts to its gently rolling farmland, from its wild moorland to its densely wooded valleys, there is always something new to explore and discover. And there is a similar pleasure of discovery in its villages – the whitewashed fishermen's cottages clinging to a cliff, cob and thatch houses hidden in the folds of a valley, granite moorland farmhouses standing four-square against the elements, Victorian hotels clustered around a popular beach.

In *Village Walks* I have tried to capture the whole spectrum of Devon's countryside. Not all the villages are of the archetypal 'whitewash-and-thatch-cottage' variety – although many are – because that is not what the county is like. With some their appeal is immediately apparent, while others hide their charms down side streets and bylanes, and need to be explored. But all have one thing in common: they all reflect the landscapes from which they have sprung. In a similar way, I have tried to select walks that capture the quality of the area. Some offer outstanding views, some stunning scenery and others delightful riverside or woodland trails – while some manage to include a bit of everything!

There are simple but clear route descriptions for each walk, with sketch maps as a further aid. If you want more detail, the numbers of the relevant Ordnance Survey maps are given. The 1:50,000 Landranger series is the most common, but some of the especially popular areas – Dartmoor, Exmoor, South Devon and the Torquay-Dawlish and Exmouth-Sidmouth areas – are covered by more detailed 1:25,000 Outdoor Leisure or Explorer maps.

For each walk there are details of where you can obtain refreshments – usually a pub, but sometimes a tearoom or restaurant. Most are in the villages themselves, but where there are places along the route of the walk I say so. I have tried to give an idea of the range of food on offer, but of course menus change, in some cases daily, so if you have any special requirements it would be as well to ring before you go (telephone numbers are given for those establishments I particularly recommend).

In each instance there is also information on where to park. In many cases this will be a public car park, but in some villages the only parking is in the street. If this is the case, please ensure that you park with consideration for the local residents – do not block any entrances (including farm gates) or obstruct any bottlenecks in the road. Most of the pubs have car parks, but remember that these are for patrons only. If you are visiting the pub there is usually no problem about leaving your car in the car park while you walk, but do ask first.

For those who fancy making a day of it, I give a brief outline of places worth visiting in the vicinity of each village. These range from an Iron Age hill fort to the latest theme parks, and include stately homes, miniature railways, museums, wildlife parks, farms and a host of other attractions for young and old.

It is important to your enjoyment of walking, and to your safety, that you are appropriately dressed. For your feet I strongly recommend walking boots or stout shoes. Boots are better at providing ankle support, which is important when you are walking over rough ground, and if you can waterproof your footwear it will prevent your feet becoming too wet – remember that even walking across a grassy field can soak them if it has been raining, or if the dew has been particularly heavy. Smooth soles should never be worn; they can be very dangerous on rough or wet ground. It is also useful to take waterproofs with you even if it is fine when you set out; you can never be sure that it will stay fine all the time you are out, particularly in the moorland areas, where the weather is somewhat fickle. A small rucksack is ideal for carrying them, and for other small items you may want to have with you, such as binoculars or a camera.

I very much hope you enjoy exploring the hidden – and not so hidden – corners of this beautiful county as much as I have. Happy walking!

Michael Bennie

Acknowledgements

I am very grateful to my son Jonathan, who drew the maps for this book and who accompanied me on several of the walks. I would also like to thank the people of the villages I visited, who were unfailingly courteous and helpful, and the many farmers and landowners I met, who were always ready with a cheery greeting and a few timely directions whenever they came across me wandering over their land.

LEE

Length : 4¹/₂ miles

Getting there: As you pass through Ilfracombe on the A361 road towards Barnstaple, you will see Lee signposted off to the right. Coming from the other direction, turn left off the A361 onto the B3343 to	Woolacombe, and then turn right, following the signposts for Lee. **Parking:** The best car park for this walk is the one alongside the village hall at the top of the village, but if	that is full there is another at the bottom. **Map:** OS Landranger 180 Barnstaple and Ilfracombe (GR 485462).

This stretch of the North Devon coast was notorious in the past as the haunt of smugglers and wreckers – the former bringing in a wide range of goods, but mainly gin and brandy, and the latter leading unsuspecting ships to destruction on the rocky shore – and Lee was the home of one of the most notorious, one Hannibal Richards.

There is little sign of this violent past in the beautiful, quiet village we see today. Its colour-washed old cottages straggle down

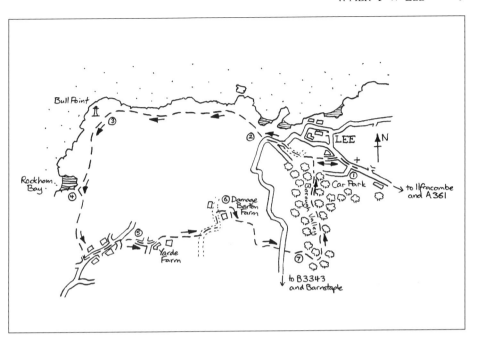

the hill to the rocks of Lee Bay, with gracious houses lining the road on the other side. The village inn, the Grampus, is one of the oldest buildings hereabouts – about 400 years old – although it was originally a farm. About the same age is the old mill by the water's edge, now a private residence, while the old post office dates back to 1706.

The walk leads you through the village to the sea, and then along the South West Coast Path, from where you get a good view of the treacherous rocks which were the death of so many ships (and men) in the past. This stretch is very hilly, with the path sweeping down to cross the occasional stream and then climbing steeply up out of the valley again, but the views when you reach the cliffs are spectacular.

The return journey is much easier, initially along farm paths and tracks, and then down through the beautiful woods of Borough Valley back to Lee.

THE WALK

❶   Across the road from the village hall car park, next to the 19th-century church, is the old school room, now an art and craft centre. To start the walk, turn left as you leave the car park. At the road junction, where you see the sign for the Grampus Inn, go left, and follow the lane until it ends. Then follow the footpath across a small bridge and between two fences to a track. You will see the attractive gardens of the Lee Bay Hotel over on your right. The track comes out onto a road; turn left and follow the road up the hill out of the village.

❷   Soon you will see a coastal footpath sign pointing to the right through a gate.

The village hall at Lee.

Turn off the road here and follow the path up through a field onto Damage Cliffs, one of many stretches of this coastline owned by the National Trust. If you look back here, you get a lovely view up the valley to Lee

---

FOOD and DRINK

The Grampus Inn (telephone: 01271 862906) is a delightful old pub with an attractive garden, which serves a wide range of snacks and main meals both midday and evenings. Alternatively you might try the Fuchsia Tea Gardens (telephone: 01271 863551) for teas, coffees and light snacks. You pass both of these establishments on the walk. You also pass the little village shop, where you can buy the makings of a picnic.

---

and also along the coast. The path leads you down into a couple of valleys and out again, across footbridges and over stiles, and with each climb the view back along the coast improves, giving you an excellent excuse to stop and catch your breath!

❸   About a mile after joining the coast path, you pass Bull Point and its lighthouse. Keep to the path along the edge of the cliff, crossing the track to the lighthouse. About $1/2$ mile beyond Bull Point you pass Rockham Bay. As you do so, you will see a clear path going left away from the bay; ignore it, and carry on up the hill beyond.

❹   About 200 yards past Rockham Bay,

you will see a path branching off to the left. Take that and you will come to a gate marked 'footpath to North Morte Farm'. Go through and follow the path up a field to a camping and caravan site. Bear right to a track, and at the junction go right again, through the caravan park, to a road. Turn left.

❺ Just before the gate leading to the track to Bull Point lighthouse, turn right up the drive for Easewell Farm, which is signposted 'footpath to Lee'. The drive takes you through another campsite, with excellent views across the undulating farmland, to a cluster of buildings (toilets, a restaurant etc). Make your way among them, following the footpath signs. Once past the buildings, you go through a gate, across a small field, over a stile and round to the left past Yarde Farm. The path follows a broad track between high hedges. At the end you cross a stile into a field. Keep to the left across two fields until you reach a track. Turn left and follow the track down and round Damage Barton farm.

❻ The track ends at a gate, where you turn right, following the footpath sign. After a few yards, turn left, as indicated by the yellow waymark. At the top of the field, go right, again following the yellow waymark. A few yards further on, there is a fingerpost giving you a choice of two paths. Take the right-hand one, and follow the waymarks and footpath signs across several fields to a road. Cross the road and bear right to cross the field on the other side to a stile and into the woods above Borough Valley.

❼ Go down the steep path among the trees to the valley floor, and then turn left along another path, signposted to Lee. This leads you down alongside a stream, through a gorgeous wood carpeted with wild flowers in season. At the end, you cross a small field to join the footpath you went out on. Turn right, cross the footbridge and make your way back to the car park.

COMBE MARTIN

Length : 4¹/₂ miles

<table>
</table>

Getting there: The village is on the A399, about 4¹/₂ miles east of Ilfracombe. Parking: There is a free car park near the church, towards the top of the village, and a couple of pay	and display car parks at the bottom, near the bay. You can use either, as the route of the walk passes both, but the area around the bay is the 'heart' of the village and the most attractive area, so I prefer to pay for the privilege	of parking there. Maps: OS Landranger 180 Barnstaple and Ilfracombe; OS Outdoor Leisure 9 Exmoor (GR 578472).

Situated right on the edge of Exmoor, Combe Martin's history stretches back to the 11th century; it is mentioned in the Domesday Book. The mainstay of the local economy in the Middle Ages was silver mining, supplemented by limestone quarry-ing, and it was a market town with the right to hold an annual fair.

Little is left to remind the visitor of this history. There are the remains of a 12th-century manor hall in Castle Street, and the lovely wagon-roofed church has a

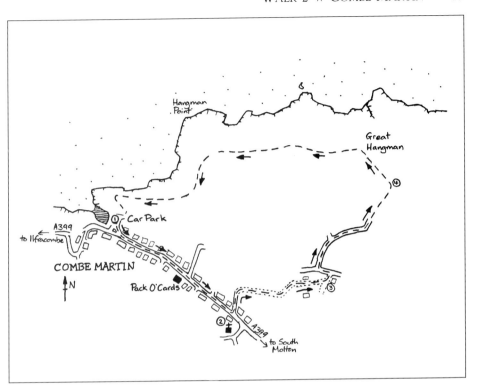

13th-century chancel. You might also like to investigate the epitaphs in the churchyard – many of them make interesting reading. And a little way down the village's long main street (at over 2 miles reputed to be the longest in England) is the Pack O' Cards pub, a 17th-century building erected by George Ley to celebrate his gambling successes. It has four floors to represent the four suits in a card pack, 13 doors on each floor for the cards in each suit, and it originally had 52 windows to represent the total number of cards in the pack.

Despite its lack of ancient buildings, however, Combe Martin is still a delightful place – an interesting blend of holiday village and working community. Victorian houses, now mainly hotels and guest houses, line the main street, and the area around the cove at the bottom of the street is particularly attractive. There is also a wide variety of things to see and do, both in the village itself and in the surrounding area.

The walk takes you through the village and then climbs up into the Exmoor National Park, following farm paths and tracks to the open moorland. You return along the coast, with superb views all around, before dipping down to the bay and the village again.

THE WALK

These directions assume that you are starting from the bottom of the village. If you have parked by the church, then you

The view along the coast from Great Hangman.

can start immediately opposite it and finish with the walk up the main street.

❶ You start with a gentle amble up the main street of the village (its name changes from time to time, but you are unlikely to notice), enjoying the holiday ambience and admiring the Victorian terraces along the way. After about ¹/₂ mile you pass the Pack O' Cards on your right.

❷ About 500 yards beyond the Pack O' Cards, you will see the church set back from the road on the right. Turn left opposite it, up Corner Lane. At the top, beyond the houses, the lane becomes no more than a track. Keep following it up a steep hill and

round to the right. When you eventually emerge from the trees, you get a very good view of the patchwork of fields over the valley as you continue climbing. Near the top of the hill you join a surfaced track and a little further on there is a T-junction. Since this is the top of the hill, you might like to pause and catch your breath. As you do so, look back and you will see a superb panorama which makes the climb seem almost worth while!

❸ Turn left onto the new track, and at the T-junction a few yards further on, turn left again onto a road. After another few yards, turn right down a track marked with National Trust signs. You are now in the

---

FOOD and DRINK

Combe Martin is extremely well served with a wide variety of places to eat and drink. There are also several shops selling ice cream, as well as everything you need to make up a picnic. The Pack O' Cards inn (telephone: 01271 882300) is worth a visit, not just out of interest but also because it serves a wide variety of excellent fare, ranging from cream teas to bar snacks and main meals. It also has a beautiful garden and a children's adventure playground. At the bottom of the village, the Fo'c'sle Inn (telephone: 01271 883354) offers a range of dishes, from jacket potatoes to the more exotic Butterfly Chicken Texas Style, which you can enjoy overlooking the bay. If tearooms are what you are after there are several in the main street, and my choice is the Zilver Spoon Restaurant (telephone: 01271 883568), which you pass on your way up the village.

Exmoor National Park. Ignore the path off to the left about 200 yards down the track,

---

PLACES of INTEREST

Just next to the lower car park is the **Combe Martin Motorcycle Collection**, an interesting little museum for motor enthusiasts, while on the outskirts of the village the **Combe Martin Wildlife and Dinosaur Park** is a delight for the children, combining real animals such as sealions, monkeys and otters with models of dinosaurs. A little further afield, 3 miles towards Ilfracombe, is **Watermouth Castle**, another children's paradise, with haunted mills and dungeons. South of Combe Martin you will find **Bodstone Barton Farm Park** (3 miles), which offers pony rides as well as the chance to see the usual range of farm animals, the **Exmoor Zoological Park** (8 miles), whose speciality is exotic birds, and for steam enthusiasts, the **Exmoor Steam Railway** (9 miles). And on the A39 to Barnstaple (6 miles from Combe Martin) is the National Trust property of **Arlington Court**, renowned for its garden.

---

which is signposted to Combe Martin, and carry straight on, following the sign to Great Hangman. Keep to the right of the house called Girt Down to a gate and keep following the track on the other side. It takes you through two gates and then peters out in the field beyond. Cross the field to a stile leading out onto an area of open moorland, and follow the wall on your right.

❹   Where the wall veers to the right, turn left onto a clear, broad path. This is the South West Coast Path. It takes you past the cairn of Great Hangman, the view from which will take your breath away – a 360° sweep, with Wales across the Bristol Channel to the north, rolling farmland to the south and the rugged coastline to the east and west. You then follow the edge of the cliff for just over a mile to Hangman Point. You can climb the point for a better view if you wish, but the main path bypasses it. Keep following the path as it hugs the coastline, and you will come to a shelter with a couple of benches. Just beyond it, where the path forks by a National Trust sign, go left and you will come out just above the car park at the bottom of the village.

LYNMOUTH

Length : 4 miles

Getting there: Lynmouth is on the A39 between Minehead and Barnstaple.	Parking: There is a pay and display car park right at the bottom of the village, beyond the harbour.	Maps: OS Landranger 180 Barnstaple and Ilfracombe; OS Outdoor Leisure 9 Exmoor (GR 720497)

The area around Lynmouth and its twin village at the top of the cliff, Lynton, was called the little Switzerland of England in the 19th century because of its magnificent scenery and quiet charm, and it was very popular among Victorian holidaymakers. It has lost none of its charm and appeal since then, despite the disaster of 1952, when the East and West Lyn rivers flooded the village, killing 31 people and destroying 93 houses.

Enough of the original buildings remain or have been restored to make this one of the prettiest coastal villages in Devon. Its hub is the tidal harbour, with the interesting Rhenish Tower on the west jetty – a replica of one which was destroyed in the flood, and which served as a beacon for

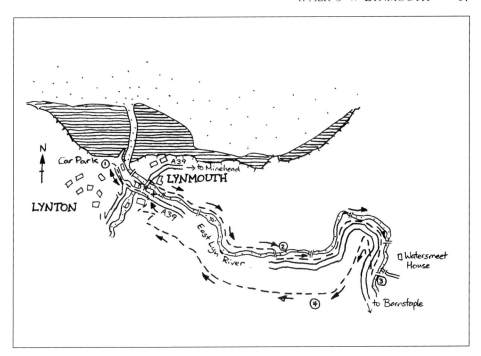

local sailors. The other main feature of the harbourside is the unusual water-operated cliff railway, built in 1890, which links Lynmouth and Lynton.

The poet Shelley had links with the village. He is believed to have stayed in Shelley's Cottage, opposite the church, and some of his writing was done here, including some pamphlets which were regarded as seditious by the government of the time. Shelley just managed to avoid arrest by taking a boat to Wales.

Perhaps the most beautiful feature of the village, however, is the valley of the East Lyn river, with houses and hotels clinging to the steep and densely wooded slopes. And that is where this route takes you – up the valley, through cool, green woodland, to Watersmeet, and then back over the area known as the Cleaves, sometimes contouring round the steep hillsides, sometimes climbing up and down them, but always with excellent views.

THE WALK

❶ As you leave the car park, you pass the cliff railway on your right. Follow the road round to the right, and you will see the Rhenish Tower on the jetty to your left. At the T-junction, turn left to cross the East Lyn river, then immediately right up Tors Road. At the fork, go right. The road passes alongside the river, with some very attractive stone cottages on the left. When it ends, continue along the surfaced path, following the sign to Watersmeet. With the river cascading down over the rocks on the right, and the dense woodland all around, this is an idyllic stretch – and you can continue to enjoy it for about 1¹/₂ miles.

The East Lyn at Watersmeet.

❷ About ³⁄₄ mile after leaving Lynmouth, the path crosses the river via a wooden footbridge and continues up the valley on the other side. After another ¹⁄₂ mile you join a track. Follow that for a short distance until it bends left to cross the river. If you want to visit Watersmeet House, a Victorian fishing lodge which is now a National Trust shop and tea garden, then follow it round; if not, carry straight on along a path.

❸ Just beyond Watersmeet House, turn sharp right, almost back on yourself, following the signpost to Lynton via the Cleaves. The path climbs to a road; cross

over, following the signpost to Lynmouth and Lynbridge via the Cleaves. There is a steep but mercifully short climb up through the woods to a patch of open ground, in the middle of which are the remains of an Iron Age camp. Carry on past it and up the next hill, which is steeper than the last but made easier by steps. Stop from time to time as you go up, as the views get better and better, both up and down the valley.

❹ At the top, the path contours round the hill and you get a clear view right down the valley to the sea. You go through two gates and the path winds down to cross a stream, and then winds up the other side. At the top there is another gorgeous view

FOOD and DRINK

There are several cafés and tearooms to choose from in Lynmouth, and two inns serving pub meals – the Village Inn and the Bath Hotel. The place that offers the best combination of situation and food, however, is the Cornerhouse Restaurant (telephone: 01598 753300). It is right by the river, with a most attractive garden, and offers a wide range of pasties, snacks and meals (mainly grills), as well as cream teas, coffee and so on. But I have to say that my own preference is to wait until I reach Watersmeet. The National Trust tearoom at Watersmeet House (telephone: 01598 753348) is in an idyllic setting, with a garden stretching down to the river, and offers a range of wholesome soups and snacks such as quiche and ploughman's lunch, as well as cream teas. If you prefer to picnic, the shops in Lynmouth will be able to supply you with what you need, while at Rocklyn Tea Gardens, which you pass on your way up the valley, you can get a delicious range of filled rolls.

up the valley of the East Lyn, and then as you round the hill you can look down on Lynmouth and along the coast. At the fork in the path, go right (signposted to Lynmouth), and at the next fork right again. This path takes you into the woods of Lyn Cleave, winding steeply down the side of the hill. At the bottom it twists and turns among some pretty cottages and finally ends at a road. Turn left, cross the main road and turn left again, down Riverside Road, to return to the car park.

PLACES of INTEREST

In Lynmouth itself, you can visit the **Woodside Craft Centre** and the **Exmoor Brass Rubbing Centre**, while a trip on the **cliff railway** up to Lynton is an interesting experience. While you are in Lynton, visit the **Lyn and Exmoor Museum**, with displays of the tools and the work of local craftsmen. And just the other side of Lynton is the **Valley of Rocks**, a fascinating area containing rocks which have weathered into the strangest formations.

CLOVELLY

Length : 3¹/₄ miles

Getting there: The B3237 runs north from the A39 between Bideford and Bude straight to Clovelly.	Parking: Cars are not allowed in the village, so the only parking is in the car park at the top of the hill.	Map: OS Landranger 190 Bude, Clovelly and surrounding area (GR 315249).

The sign at the entrance to Clovelly describes it as 'one of the world's unique villages', and although 'unique' is one of the most misused words in the English language, in this case the description is apt. It is a beautifully preserved fishing village clinging to the cliffs along its single cobbled street (called Up-Along or Down-Along, depending on which way you are going).

But it is not only its beauty which makes Clovelly unique. The whole village is owned in feudal style by one person, the Hon John Rouse, and at the entrance is the Clovelly Centre which contains a restaurant, a shop and an audio-visual display for those who are put off by the steepness of the village street. Indeed, the only way into Clovelly is through the Centre, and there is an entrance charge of approximately £2. And if this makes it sound too much like a 'theme park' village for your liking, take heart. The climbing and the entrance fee serve to deter the less determined visitors, and both the village and the Clovelly Centre are refreshingly free from phoney souvenirs and trinkets. Indeed, once through the Centre, you will find Clovelly to be a living, working community like many others, although the boats in the harbour are more likely to be waiting to take holiday-makers out than unloading fish. And although it can become crowded in the summer season, it nevertheless retains its unselfconscious charm.

The route takes you round the coast from the village, through some lovely woodland, and then returns past the interesting church. Apart from the climb down and then back up the village street, it is an easy route, and full of interest.

THE WALK

❶ Go through the Clovelly Centre and follow the path on the other side. When you have finished exploring the village, return up the street. Alternatively, you can turn right up North Hill for a different route back. If you follow the street, you will come to a grassy area with a memorial cross on your right at the top, with a sign indicating that this is the entrance to the National Trust property of Mount Pleasant. Turn right here. If you go up North Hill, the path will bring you out at the same area, and you should bear right along the cliff-top.

❷ This path brings you out at the road where the Land Rovers shuttle people who cannot manage the climb to and from the village. Cross over the road to a large gate marked with the acorn sign of the Coast Path. Go through and bear right along a track which runs parallel to the road below. It takes you round into a wood, with glimpses of the sea through the trees on your right, and then out into a field. A succession of kissing gates lead you back into the wood, out into another field and into the wood once again. This is a lovely

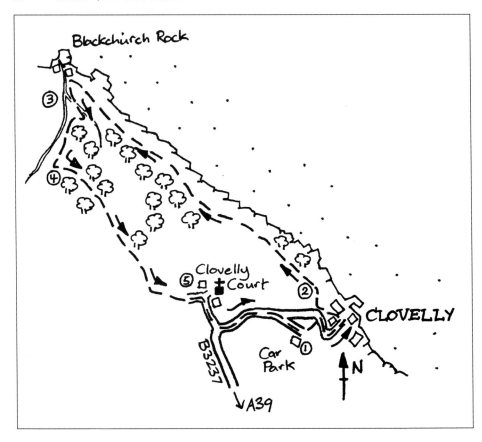

stretch of woodland, filled with wild flowers at all times of the year. When you come to a

---

FOOD and DRINK

There are two hostelries in Clovelly: the Red Lion Hotel (telephone: 01237 431237) by the quay and the New Inn (telephone 01237 431303) halfway down the village. Both are good, but perhaps the New Inn has the edge. It is a very atmospheric pub, with a good range of food, from snacks to main meals such as cottage pie, fisherman's pie and lasagne. The Cottage Tearoom provides cream teas and a variety of rolls and light meals, and the post office sells pasties and groceries.

---

junction in the path, go right, following the Coast Path sign, rather than left back to the church. You then come to a track, both sides of which are marked 'No public access'. Go half right away from it, following the Coast Path sign. This path takes you through a clearing filled with bracken and wild flowers, and then you begin to descend quite steeply. The path eventually ends at a track. Turn right, then sharp left and sharp right again in quick succession, to follow another track down towards the sea, with Lundy Island clearly visible ahead of you.

❸ Follow the track sharply round to the

Clovelly Court.

left. At the fork, go right to cross a stream, then continue along the track as it winds up to the right and then to the left.

❹ About 500 yards after crossing the stream you will see a public bridleway sign on your left. Turn up here onto another track, which leads to a gate. Keep to the left of the field beyond to another gate. Go through it and turn right. Keep to the right of this field, and at the top go left to follow the field boundary to a gate onto a track. Go through yet another gate and follow the track through a farmyard to a lane.

❺ Follow the lane as it winds past Clovelly Court and then the church on

the left to a gateway. Go through onto the road, turn left, and the turning for the car park is about 300 yards further on, on your right.

PLACES of INTEREST

The Milky Way and North Devon Bird of Prey Centre, 2 miles away, combines all the attractions of a farm park (including what is advertised as Europe's largest 'cuddling corner') with slides, rides and activities, and falconry flying displays. A little further afield, 6 miles away, is the 12th-century **Hartland Abbey**, which contains exhibitions of period furniture and porcelain.

WALK 5
APPLEDORE
Length : 5 miles

Getting there: Take the A386 north from Bideford.

Parking: There are two pay and display car parks in Appledore; the most convenient for this walk is the one by the shore at the end of The Quay, but if that is full there is another in Odun Road, higher up the village, opposite the North Devon Maritime Museum.

Map: OS Landranger 180 Barnstaple and Ilfracombe (GR 463307).

Appledore is steeped in maritime history: shipbuilding, seafaring, ropemaking and, of course, smuggling have all played a major part in its development over the centuries. Indeed, it still has a shipyard today. In 1588 it became a free port in recognition of the part its ships and men played in the defeat of the Spanish Armada and ships used to land tobacco and cod from America here.

The Quay, right on the shore, is the hub of the village, with attractive narrow streets of Elizabethan and Georgian houses and cottages leading off it. And if you explore some of these side streets, you will often find fascinating little courts tucked away off them.

Irsha Street, one such side lane, is particularly picturesque, and this walk takes you along it before leaving the village to visit Northam Burrows, an interesting area of dunes and salt marshes which juts into Bideford Bay. Unlike many coastal walks in this area there is virtually no climbing, but you nevertheless get some very good views.

THE WALK

❶ If you have parked in Odun Road, then go back to the main road and follow it down to the shore and to The Quay to join the main route. If you have parked at the end of The Quay, then leave the car park at the far (north-western) end. Instead of following

the main road up the hill, take Irsha Street, the narrow lane that branches off to the right. It is a very attractive little street of close-packed houses, with courts and slip-ways leading off it.

❷ At the end of the street is the lifeboat station. Immediately before you reach it, go left up some steps to a path. The path comes out at a road; turn right and follow the road out of the village, continuing for about ¹/₂ mile.

❸ At the crossroads in the little hamlet of Watertown, turn right, following the Coast Path sign. The road takes you to the Northam Burrows Country Park. Once in the park, you can more or less wander at will, but it is best to keep to the line of the road initially, as it hugs the coast. There are superb views across the estuary to the right and along the coast to the left. The Burrows themselves are an interesting mixture of grassy dunes and salt marshes, and are home to a variety of bird and insect life. When the road bends to the right, leave it and go straight on, keeping the wooden fence which surrounds one of the dunes to your right.

❹ Make your way through the dunes to the aptly named Pebble Ridge. This natural barrier runs for some distance along the

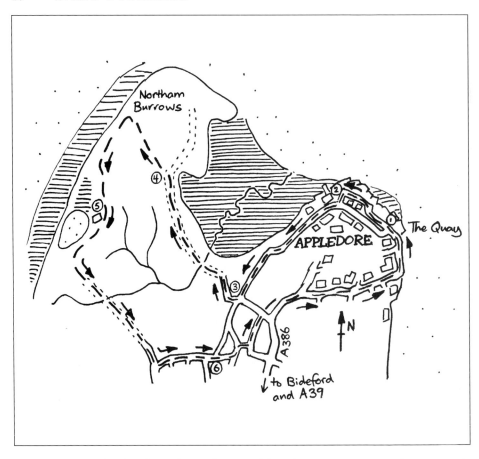

coast between the beach and Northam Burrows. The area presents some interesting features: there is the ridge of pebbles

---

FOOD and DRINK

There are a number of pubs and tearooms to choose from in Appledore, and shops that can sell you the makings of a picnic. I can especially recommend the Beaver Inn (telephone: 01237 474822), which is in Irsha Street, on the route of the walk and right by the shore. It offers the usual range of bar snacks, but also a mouthwatering selection of seafood, including butterfly king prawns, calamari and skate wings.

(although most are quite large stones), then a strip of golden sand, and at the water line another accumulation of stones. Turn left and follow the ridge, with a golf course on your left and the beach on your right. If you find it difficult walking across the stones, you can go down to the sand and follow the beach or slightly inland to skirt the golf course. Personally I am fascinated by the colours, patterns and shapes of the stones, so I prefer to follow the ridge. After about 500 yards or so, you will come to a path leading off to the left between wooden fences, marked with a yellow-topped post.

North Devon Maritime Museum, Appledore.

PLACES of INTEREST

In Appledore itself there is the **North Devon Maritime Museum**, with an interesting collection of nautical exhibits. About 4 miles along the A39 towards Bude is the **Big Sheep**, a farm park with a wide variety of attractions for young children, including sheep racing!

Turn left and follow it to the golf course. Turn right along the edge of the course, following the line of yellow-topped posts.

❺   You will soon come to an information centre, which contains a great deal of information about the natural history of the Burrows and about Charles Kingsley, who lived in the area. Just beyond the information centre you come to a road. Follow it and ahead of you you will see the resort of Westward Ho! This village was constructed in Victorian times in an attempt to attract trade away from the South Devon resorts, and was named after the Kingsley novel, exclamation mark and all. When the road forks, go left. Leave the country park and take the first turning on the left (signposted to Appledore). You pass a new housing development on your right, just beyond which is a road called Highbury Hill.

❻   Just a few yards past Highbury Hill you will come to another junction. Turn half right here up a narrow lane. At the T-junction at the end turn left, and at the next junction go right and almost immediately left. When you come to another T-junction, go straight across to a path between two banks. Follow it up and it will bring you out at the main road, the A386. Turn left and follow the road back to Appledore.

NORTH MOLTON

Length : 2³/₄ miles

Getting there: North Molton lies 2½ miles north of the A361 between Tiverton and Barnstaple, and is clearly signposted from it. **Parking:** There is free	parking in The Square, up near the church, but if that is full, there is plenty of space along the main street through the village, as long as you park with consideration for local people.	**Map:** OS Landranger 180 Barnstaple and Ilfracombe (GR 737299).

Northorth Molton is an ancient village – it is difficult to be sure exactly how ancient, but there is known to have been a Neolithic settlement here and it is mentioned in the Domesday Book, so, depending on one's viewpoint, it could be said to be thousands of years old or a 'mere' 900 years. It was an important mining centre in the past, with iron, copper and silver all being extracted at some time or another.

It is a long village, stretching for about a mile from the river Mole up a hill to the church and beyond. Just off the main street is The Square, overlooked on three sides by

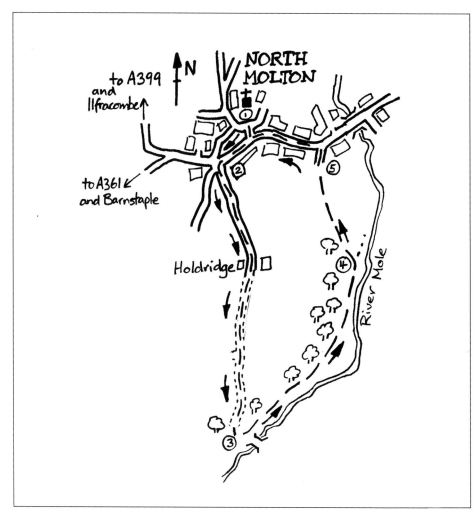

pretty houses and on the fourth by the imposing church. The long main street is lined with more attractive dwellings – solid stone cottages and whitewashed houses, all roofed with the black slate so typical of Devon.

You will find yourself walking almost the entire length of the village eventually, but in two 'bites' – part of it at the beginning of the walk and part at the end. In between, the route takes you down a deserted country lane filled with wayside flowers, along the riverside and through a beautiful, sheltering wood. It is a lovely amble at any time, but particularly in early summer, when the hedgerows are literally a mass of pink – foxgloves, red campion and rosebay willowherb all vying for attention. There is one short wet stretch, so suitable shoes or boots are recommended.

One of the attractive solid stone cottages to be seen in the village.

THE WALK

❶ Starting from The Square, make your way down to the main street and turn right. Follow the road past the post office and take the next turning on the left. It is signposted to Holdridge, but the signpost is a few yards further down the road, so you may miss it.

❷ After a few yards, turn left again (signposted to Holdridge again). This lane takes you out of the village, climbing gently as you go. It is lined by banks and hedges filled with wild flowers. As you pass a gateway on your left near the top of the hill, you get a very good view across to North Molton and the farms beyond, and then, as the lane begins to descend, another view

across the rolling fields ahead. You pass Holdridge Farm on your left and the lane

---

FOOD and DRINK

There are two pubs in North Molton, both offering a range of fare. The Poltimore Inn (telephone: 01598 740338), at the start of the walk, is a pleasant place which serves everything from cream teas to a delicious crab salad. Alternatively there is the Miners' Arms (telephone: 01598 740316), further down the road and passed towards the end of the walk, which offers delicious 'munchskins' (wedges of fried potato with a variety of toppings), as well as traditional snacks such as ploughman's lunches and main courses which include exotic Thai stir-fried chicken. There is also a grocery in the main street if you prefer to picnic.

becomes an unsurfaced track and goes down quite steeply into a wood, still between high banks.

❸   At the bottom, the lane curves sharply to the left, and as it does so you will the see a public footpath sign pointing through a gate. Go through into a clear area dotted with young trees. Follow a grassy track along the left of the area and you will meet up with the river Mole on your right. The track leads to another gate, beyond which is a wood. Carry on through the wood, with masses of wild flowers on either side. Down here near the water, you will find marsh thistle and ragged robin adding to the early summer pink celebration. The track narrows to a path and crosses another open stretch dotted with young trees, keeping to the left, at the bottom of a wood. You pass a footbridge across the river on your right, but you should continue straight on to go through a gate.

❹   Shortly after the gate, the path forks, with the more obvious route going slightly to the right along a low bank. Take the left fork, following the edge of the wood. Soon there is a slight climb to a stile leading into the wood itself. The path climbs briefly through the wood to a gate. After the gate it descends to a rather muddy patch, followed by a short stretch when you are all but paddling, as the path forms the bed of a small rivulet. The water is no more than an inch deep, however, so provided you are not wearing your best shoes there should be no problem. The path soon branches off to the left and leads you to a track. Turn right and follow the track to a road.

❺   Turn left into the road and follow it up the hill through the village to The Square.

IDDESLEIGH

Length : 4¹/₄ miles

Getting there: Iddesleigh is on the B3217 between Exbourne and Dolton.	Parking: In the road. If you are parking outside the pub, make sure that you do not block the road, as it is rather narrow.	Map: OS Landranger 191 Okehampton and North Dartmoor (GR 570082).

This is one of Devon's hidden gems – a collection of picturesque thatched cottages gathered around a green, with a beautiful old pub set back from the road and an attractive 15th-century church alongside. It is in an ideal situation, too, on the southern slopes of a spur overlooking the river Okement to the south and the Torridge to the west.

The church is worth a visit to see the angels in the chancel roof, which look down on the effigy of a 13th-century crusader. Its curate for a few years in the 1830s was the Rev Jack Russell, a famous sportsman and originator of the Jack Russell terrier. The village's other claim

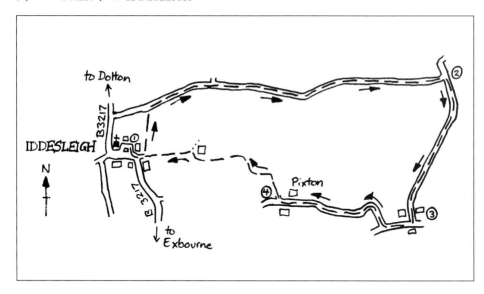

to fame is that it had an earldom named after it. Sir Stafford Northcote, whose family had owned land in the area since the 17th century, became Foreign Secretary and then Chancellor of the Exchequer in the 19th century, and when he was elevated to the peerage he took the title 'Earl of Iddesleigh'.

The main attraction of the walk is the views. There are superb panoramas from almost every point – to the south the horizon is dominated by the bleak and rugged tors of Dartmoor, and to the east, west and north you look out across the undulating grassland which is such a feature of this area, punctuated by large

---

FOOD and DRINK

The village pub is the Duke of York, a lovely old inn set back from the main road (telephone: 01837 810253). It offers a surprisingly varied menu, ranging from sandwiches, soups and salads to steaks, curries and fish dishes.

---

stretches of woodland. This is *Tarka the Otter* country, made famous by Henry Williamson's classic, and for a short distance our route follows the Tarka Trail, a long-distance walking and cycling trail which explores the areas around the rivers Taw and Torridge, where the book is set. The walk mainly follows pretty lanes, flower-filled in summer, but there are some farm paths which can become overgrown and muddy at times, so long trousers and boots are recommended.

THE WALK

❶ Starting from the pub, turn left, go down to the main road and turn left again. Almost immediately after you join the road, it turns to the right; do not follow it round, but go straight on down a track, following the Tarka Trail sign. After a few yards, turn left through a gate, following a yellow waymark. Go up the left-hand side of a field to another gate, and then go diag-

A delightful, thatched cottage near Iddesleigh.

onally right across the next field to a further gate in the far corner. If you look back, you can see right across the farms to Dartmoor

---

PLACES of INTEREST

Barometer World at Merton, about 3¹/₂ miles to the north-west, has a fascinating display of barometers from the last 300 years. Some 7 miles away, near Great Torrington, is the Royal Horticultural Society's garden at **Rosemoor**. Described as the 'Wisley of the West', it comprises 40 acres of themed gardens of all kinds, from herbs to water features. Its main attraction, however, is the superb collection of roses – some 200 varieties. In Great Torrington itself, you can visit the renowned **Dartington Crystal** works and see crystal being made.

– a view that will remain with you, with variations, for most of the walk. Go through the gate into a lane and turn right. This is a lovely lane, fringed with wild flowers in the spring and summer, and from time to time you get some good views through the hedges. Continue for about 1¹/₂ miles.

❷ When the lane turns sharply to the left, you should turn right down a side lane (signposted to Monkokehampton). The view from here is superb – a 360° panorama, with the barren wastes of Dartmoor on the horizon to the south, and farms and woods rolling away into the distance to the north, east and west. The lane takes you down into a valley and up the other side, and about a mile after joining it you come to a T-junction.

❸   Turn right here (signposted to Monkokehampton again), and 200 yards further on go right again down another lane (signposted to Pixton). After about ³/₄ mile you come to a farm on your right and a pretty whitewashed cottage on your left.

❹   Immediately beyond them is a public footpath sign on the right, pointing through a gate. Go through the gate onto a path between high banks. It can become overgrown, and also muddy in places, but it is quite passable. The path leads you down alongside a wood on the right and crosses a stream. On the other side it goes to the left to a gate. Keep to the hedge on the right-hand side of the field beyond, and after 100 yards or so you will find a gate on your right. Go through it and cross another little stream. Go up the next field, keeping to the hedge on the left. Follow the hedge round to the left to a gap in another hedge ahead of you, and then to a gateway at the end of the next field. This takes you onto a rough track across another field. Follow it round to the left of some farm buildings and then to the right to a gate onto a much clearer track just by the buildings. Turn left and you are back on the Tarka Trail. Follow the track back to Iddesleigh and turn right to return to the pub.

CHULMLEIGH

Length : 5½ miles

Getting there: Take the B3096 east off the A377 between Crediton and Barnstaple.	Parking: There are two free car parks just off the main street, one on each side of the church.	Map: OS Landranger 180 Barnstaple and Ilfracombe (GR 686142).

This delightful village, overlooking the valley of the Little Dart river, can trace its origins back to the Saxon period. It was a thriving centre in medieval times, and was granted two annual fairs in the 13th century, one of which continues to this day and is held at the end of July. Indeed, it is still a focal point for the area, and has a bustling air about it, even on weekday mornings. Its architecture reflects its development over the centuries, cob and thatch cottages mingling happily with Tudor merchants' houses and a few more modern buildings.

This lovely country ramble explores part of Chulmleigh's hinterland – the lush green fields, pleasant woods and quiet lanes of the Little Dart valley, one of the most

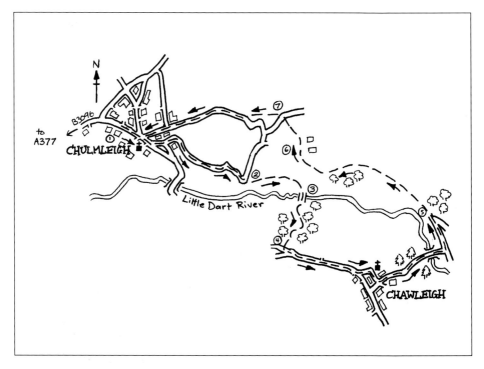

delightfully unspoilt areas of mid-Devon. What climbing there is could be described as steady rather than steep, but stout shoes or boots are recommended, as some of the paths tend to be rather muddy.

FOOD and DRINK

There are two pubs in Chulmleigh, the Red Lion and the Old Courthouse, both of which have very reasonable food. My favourite haunt, however, is the Old Bakehouse (telephone: 01769 580137), a 16th-century tearoom which, in addition to the usual tea and coffee, offers home-made soup, granary sandwiches, omelettes and a selection of main dishes. If you fancy a break in the middle of your walk, then try the Royal Oak at Chawleigh (telephone: 01769 580427), which has a wide range of snacks and main courses – their rump steak is particularly good value.

THE WALK

❶   Follow the main street south-eastwards past the Red Lion on the left and the village shops on the right. When the road bends to the right to leave the village, turn left and go past a park and children's playground. At the first junction go straight on, and at the second bear right, following the main lane out of the village. As you go, you get a good view of the rolling farmland ahead of you. The lane takes you down a steep hill to cross a stream and then goes to the left.

❷   As it does so, go straight on, through a gate, following the footpath sign. Keep to the right of the field on the other side, and at the end you will find a stile on your right. Cross it and go down some steps and across

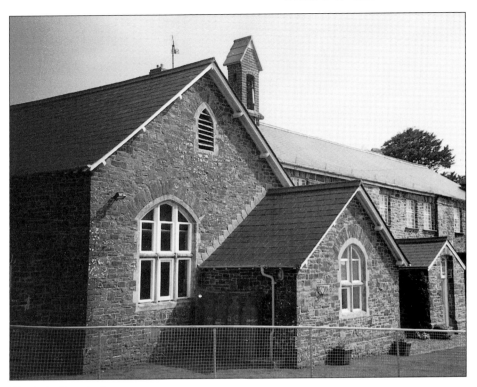

Chawleigh village school.

two footbridges into another field. Go straight across this field and through a gap in the fence to another. Bear right and follow the river, which you will see alongside you, to some steps leading up to a footbridge.

❸ Cross the bridge and follow the path straight across a field. Go through a hole in the fence into a wood and you will find a path crossing in front of you. Go right and follow the path up the hill. This is a lovely stretch of woodland, with a steep-sided valley on your left and wild flowers all around. If you are lucky, you may even see the odd deer. At the top, you go through a gate and out into a field. Follow a track up

to another gate, but do not go through it; instead, follow the track round to the left alongside a fence. This leads you through a gate onto a road.

❹ Turn left, and at the junction go straight on (signposted to Chawleigh and Witheridge). After about 200 yards you come to the outskirts of Chawleigh. Follow the road towards the centre of the village, and just before you come to the Royal Oak Inn you will see a road leading off to the left alongside some bungalows called Sunny Court. Follow that as it winds sharply to the right and then to the left past the church and the very attractive village school. At the T-junction turn left and go down to

PLACES of INTEREST

There is a **short-hole golf course** on the very edge of the village for those with an inclination in that direction. At Eggesford, 4 miles to the south, is **Eggesford Gardens**, a combined garden centre and country park.

cross the Little Dart river again. At the junction on the other side of the bridge, follow the main road round to the left (signposted to Gidley Arms).

❺   When the road turns sharply to the right, go straight on up a track. You get a very good view of woods and farmland up the valley. The track climbs up the side of the valley and near the top it forks. Take the left fork to pass the houses on your right and then cross a farmyard. At the end, go through a gate and then bear left down a track which leads into a wood, skirting the top of it. Look out for pheasants along this stretch. At the end of the wood, go through

a gate, across a track and through another gate onto a path between banks. At the end of the path is another gate leading into a field. Go straight across the field to yet another gate (**not** to the gate in the right-hand corner of the field, which leads up to a farm). Go straight on from the gate, along a grassy track between hedges. It can become a little muddy as it climbs to the right and then to the left to a farm track.

❻   Cross the track to a gate and follow the path, again between hedges, and again becoming somewhat muddy, up a hill to a road.

❼   Cross the road to a footpath sign on the other side and go over a stile into a field. Go half left down the field to another stile and make your way straight across the next field to a gate leading onto a road. Turn right and follow the road across the stream and up a hill to return to Chulmleigh.

WALK 9

CULMSTOCK

Length : 3¹/₂ miles

Getting there: Culmstock is on the B3391 which runs south-east from the A38 to Hemyock. If approaching on the M5 leave at junction 27 and follow the A38 towards Wellington. Turn right on to the B3391 and follow the signs to Culmstock.	**Parking:** Parking is possible in various places along the road through the village, but it is a fairly busy thoroughfare so please ensure that you do not cause a bottleneck by leaving your car in an awkward position; the best place to park for this walk is	probably outside the church. **Maps:** OS Landranger 181 Minehead and Brendon Hills or 193 Taunton and Lyme Regis (GR 102135).

Culmstock straddles the river Culm, with pretty traditional cob and thatch cottages interspersed with more modern housing. It was once an important cloth-making centre, and the old mill – now very tastefully converted into flats – still stands on the northern side of the village.

A fascinating feature of the church is the yew tree which grows from the top of the tower, its roots firmly embedded in the masonry. It is believed to be over 250 years old, and is so popular with the villagers that during times of drought they carry water all the way up the tower to keep it alive!

Another interesting feature of Culmstock is the beehive-shaped beacon hut on top of a hill overlooking the village. It housed one of a string of beacons positioned on prominent hillsides to warn of the approach of the Spanish Armada in the 16th century, and is believed to be the only surviving one of its type in the country. Farm paths lead you up to it, taking in a pretty riverside amble on the way. At the top you get commanding views of the surrounding countryside, and then you return via quiet country lanes.

THE WALK

❶ Starting from the church, follow the road east away from the centre of the village. Just beyond the church, turn off the main road to follow a lane round to the left. At the bottom, by a pretty thatched cottage, go right along a track. There is a public footpath sign, but it is somewhat dilapidated and hidden by a hedge. Follow the path at the end of the track to a stile and bear left towards the river. Cross a double stile and turn sharp right to follow the river upstream. Cross another double stile and make your way across the field beyond to a footbridge.

❷ Cross over the footbridge and bear left to a stile in the corner of the field. Follow the path on the other side to a road and turn right. After a short distance, turn left through a gate, following the footpath sign. Keep the hedge on your left until it veers away to the left, and then cut straight across to a stile. Follow the path on the other side until you reach a farmyard.

❸ Turn right onto a lane through the farmyard, then almost immediately left and right again, following first a yellow waymark and then a public footpath sign. Go through the gate and turn left again, to follow the hedge straight up the field. In the next field, do not carry straight on towards the trees ahead but bear right to a

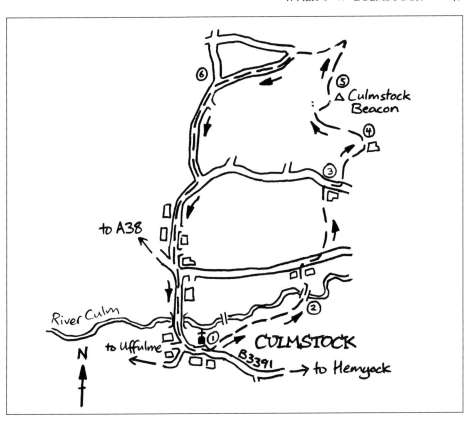

stile hidden in a hedge, with a gate just beyond. Go over the stile and through the gate; be careful as you cross the small stretch between the two as it is somewhat overgrown. Go straight up the field beyond the gate to a farm, skirting round to the left of the buildings to reach a gate onto a track.

❹ Turn left and follow the track, which leads you back into the field you have just left. A path takes you across the top of it and over a stile into a small copse. It contours round to the left of a small hill and you get a good view across the valley. Go through a gate and bear right to make your way through the bracken straight up the hill. The bracken is quite tall and thick, but the path is fairly clear as it winds up. You soon come to a much clearer path running across in front of you. Turn right and follow the path round until it meets a track. Turn left to the beacon hut.

❺ The views from up here are quite stunning, with the hills rolling away into the distance and the river winding down below you. When you have had your fill, continue along the track until it joins another. Turn left and follow the new track down into a copse, through a gate and onto a road. At the junction, turn left to continue along a lane.

The beehive-shaped beacon hut overlooking the village.

❻ At the T-junction at the end of the lane, go left again (signposted to Culmstock). This takes you down into the village.

FOOD and DRINK

There are two pubs in Culmstock: the Ilminster Stage just opposite the church and the Culm Valley Inn on the other side of the river. The Culm Valley Inn (telephone: 01884 840354) wins my vote by a short head. It has an attractive garden by the river, and offers a range of food, from bar snacks to steak and fish dishes. Pasties, pies, fruit and other picnic ingredients are available from the post office, which doubles as a village shop.

PLACES of INTEREST

At Uffculme, 2^1/$_2$ miles away, is the **Coldharbour Industrial Museum**, a working woollen mill. Just 2 miles in the other direction, near Hemyock, you will find the ruins of **Hemyock Castle**, of medieval origin.

At the junction go straight on. The old mill is just off to your left 100 yards or so before the bridge. Cross the bridge and go past the post office before turning left to return to the church.

WALK 10

SHEEPWASH

Length : 5¹/₄ miles

Getting there: Sheepwash is 1¹/₂ miles north of the A3072 Hatherleigh to Holsworthy road. Turn off at Highampton.

Parking: In the village square.

Maps: OS Landranger 191 Okehampton and North

Dartmoor (start and finish) and 190 Bude, Clovelly and surrounding area (middle section) (GR 486063).

Sheepwash is a compact little village of whitewashed thatched and slate-roofed cottages which has been declared a conservation area. Its four pretty streets converge on a central square, which still has the old village pump and is bounded by the pub, the church and the village shop.

It is Saxon in origin and was once an important market town, but a fire in 1743 caused considerable devastation and the market was transferred elsewhere. As a result it is now a sleepy, tranquil village which seems to have more tractors than cars. It is also very popular with the angling fraternity, who come to try their luck in the nearby river Torridge.

The walk shows you the rich and varied landscape of the surrounding countryside at its best, combining farm paths, woodland trails, flower-lined tracks and quiet country lanes. You pass a magnificent old manor house along the way, and some of the views are outstanding.

THE WALK

❶ Turn right (north) from the square. You pass a farm called Old Court on the left and then another farm on the right. Just beyond it you will see a public footpath sign on the left. Go through a gate and turn right to follow the edge of a field to another gate. Keep to the right of the next field, with a good view across the rolling farmland and woods on your left. Go through a third gate and continue along the right-hand edge of the next field to a stile. Go straight across the next field to a footbridge and keep to the left of the next to a gate onto a track which leads you to a road.

❷ Cross the road to another track between hedges, with another good view across to the left. It goes to the right and the left and then to the right again past a farm, where it joins another, more well-defined track; go straight on. Ignore the track that leads off to the left to Blackmoat Farm and carry on past some houses on the left. At the junction, follow the main track round to the left and then to the right, following the direction indicated by a public footpath sign. Cross a stream and enter a wood. At the T-junction, turn right. There are rhododendrons in profusion on your left and the track is fringed with rosebay willowherb in summer. The wood opens up on the left to reveal a field and just

beyond, where it closes in again, you come to a road.

❸ Turn left and follow the road through the wood and out into open country, climbing steadily as you go. Ignore the public bridleway going right just beyond the wood and follow the road on to Buckland Filleigh.

❹ You will see an old manor house on your left. This is Buckland Manor; it was a school for some time, but is now once again a private home. Turn left up the drive, and at the top, where it curves right to the front of the house, turn left and then, at the edge of the lawn, right to the church gate. Go through the gate into the churchyard and turn left at the church door to reach a stile into a field. Bear right, aiming to the right of a lake, to a footbridge. Go straight on up the next field, to the right of a couple of large chestnuts, and on up the rise. At the top go right, following the clear footpath to a lane.

❺ Turn left and follow the lane up a hill. At the top you get a superb view, all the way across to Dartmoor. After about 600 yards you will come to some houses on your left, and the lane takes a sharp turn to the right.

FOOD and DRINK

The Half Moon Inn (telephone: 01409 231376) serves bar snacks at midday, with a delicious range of sandwiches, toasted sandwiches, ploughman's lunches, pasties and salads. The Mermaid Stores, across the road, stocks a range of groceries for those who would like to make up a picnic.

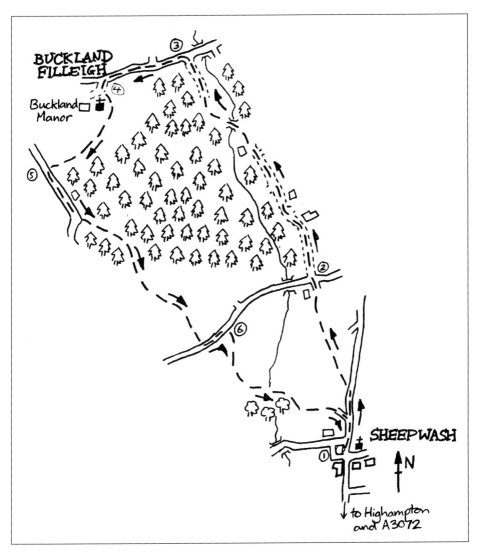

As it does so, turn left onto a track following the public footpath sign through a kissing gate. Just as the track goes to the left, turn right off it onto a path; there is a footpath sign nailed to a tree, but it is not very clear. Follow the pretty, peaceful path through the wood. Near the end it turns to the right and then leaves the wood and comes out in a field. Follow the left-hand hedge, with another excellent view of the tors of Dartmoor ahead of you, and more views across the farmland to the left and right. Go through a gap at the end of the field and continue along the left-hand hedge. Halfway down the next field you will come to a stile in the hedge on your

Buckland Manor.

left. Cross it and cut diagonally across to the right to a track in the far corner. Turn right, follow the track to a lane and turn left. Continue for about 350 yards to a farm.

❻   Turn right into the farmyard. You need to take a bit of care along this next stretch,

PLACES of INTEREST

Barometer World, at Merton (6 miles to the north-east) has a barometer museum and demonstrations of barometer making. Near Great Torrington, 8 miles away, is the Royal Horticultural Society's superb garden at **Rosemoor**: 40 acres of gardens for all tastes, including fruit, vegetables, shrubs and over 200 varieties of rose.

as there are no footpath signs or waymarks to guide you. Follow the track round to the left at the end of the farmyard and then to the right through a gate. Bear right across the field beyond towards the far corner. At the bottom, about 100 yards to the left of the corner, you will see a footbridge across a stream. Cross it and bear left to a stile. Bear left again on the other side of the stile and go up the left-hand side of a field to a line of trees running up to the right. Follow the trees to a track, which takes you through a gateway and on to a gate. Continue up the track as it twists and turns and eventually brings you past a farm to a lane. Turn right to return to Sheepwash.

MORCHARD BISHOP

Length : 3¹/₂ miles

Getting there: Morchard Bishop is about 2 miles north-east of the A377 Crediton to Barnstaple road, and is clearly signposted from both directions.

Parking: Provided you have some consideration for the local householders and avoid blocking drives and gateways, you should have no difficulty parking in the road near the centre of the village. Alternatively, if you go down towards the church and the village hall, you will find a free public car park on the edge of the village, just beyond the school. This is convenient for the end of the walk.

Map: OS Landranger 191 Okehampton and North Dartmoor (GR 770075).

The history of Morchard Bishop could be said to go back to the Iron Age, as a settlement dating from that period has been found in the area, but the origins of the present village lie in Saxon times. It is now a pleasant mixture of the old and the new strung out along its two main streets, cob and thatch rubbing shoulders with rendering and slate, with more modern houses on the outskirts.

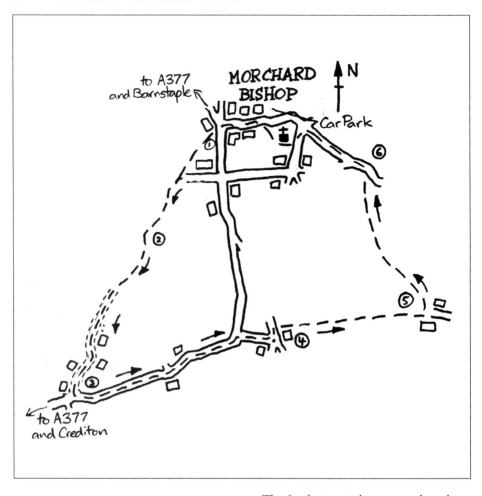

FOOD and DRINK

The only pub in the village is the 16th-century London Inn (telephone: 01363 877222), a very pleasant place to rest and slake your thirst after your walk. It also offers a good range of food, from jacket potatoes through omelettes and salads to specials like home-made lasagne and roast lamb. The village shop, across the road, can supply what you need if you want to make up a picnic.

The focal point is the crossroads and war memorial, around which are clustered the post office, the inn and the shop, with the attractive church on the edge of the village, opposite the pretty Victorian school. Just north of the post office, along the east side of Fore Street, is what is reputed to be the longest row of thatched cottages in England – a pretty chain of traditional Devon houses set back from the road in their own gardens.

The surrounding area is typical of mid-

The village school at Morchard Bishop.

Devon – lush fields scattered with wood-land – and this walk captures its essence. It follows farm paths, tracks and country lanes, with hedgerows filled with seasonal wild flowers and only the song of the birds and perhaps the distant growl of a farm tractor to disturb the peace.

THE WALK

❶ Starting from the centre of the village, follow the track almost opposite the London Inn, and at the end go left across a stile, following the footpath sign. You are now on the Two Moors Way, a long-distance path that runs from Ivybridge, on the southern edge of Dartmoor, to Lynmouth, on the north coast of Exmoor. You get a very good view across the rolling country-side ahead. Cut diagonally across the field to two gates. Go through the right-hand one, marked with the Two Moors Way waymark. Keep to the left of the next field to reach a stile, also marked with a waymark. Keep to the left again, alongside some farm buildings, and cross another stile. Follow the short track on the other side to enter another field and keep to the left again, following the hedge round.

❷ At the end, go through a gate and go left down a broad path between hedges full of wild flowers. Cross a stile and go right, still following the Two Moors Way waymark, to skirt round the next field, following the hedge round to the left at the end. Just beyond a metal gate you will find a stile on your right. Cross it and go left. As the fence turns away to the left, cut across to a gate on the other side of the field. This leads onto a grassy track between hedges, again filled with wild flowers. You come to a gate and continue along the track past some houses and a farm to a road. This is where you leave the Two Moors Way.

❸ Turn left, with the panorama of undulating fields now to your right. After ½ mile, as the road goes to the left, follow a lane straight on (signposted to Oldborough and Newbuildings).

❹ At the T-junction, go left (signposted to Morchard Bishop). You now get a good view of Morchard Bishop ahead of you. After a few yards, turn right off the road through a gate, following the footpath sign. Go straight across a field to another gate, and across the next field to a stile. Cross a stream via a small wooden footbridge and follow the left-hand side of the next field. When you come to some farm buildings, go round to the left, through a gate. Follow the fence on the right initially and then, at the corner, cut diagonally right across the field to a gate.

❺ To the left of the gate is a stile marked with a yellow arrow. Cross it and keep to the right of two fields. Go through a gate and across another field to a track. This leads you into another field and up the left-hand side. Go through the gate at the end to another track.

❻ Bear left and follow the track past a farm to a road. Cross over to a gate and cross a field to another gate leading into the churchyard. Go round the church to a road. Turn right to get to the car park, if that is where you have left your car, or left to return to the centre of the village.

DUNKESWELL
Length : 4¹/₄ miles

Getting there:
Approaching from the M5, leave at junction 27 and follow the A38 towards Wellington. Turn right and follow the B3391 to Hemyock and then follow the signs to Dunkeswell. Alternatively, turn north off the A30 at Honiton and follow the signs. The village can also be reached from the A373 Honiton to Cullompton road via Awliscombe, Broadhembury or Kerswell.

Parking: There is limited parking along the narrow lanes in the village itself. There is more space along the main road which skirts the village to the west, especially opposite the Royal Oak Inn.

Maps: OS Landranger 192 Exeter and Sidmouth or 193 Taunton and Lyme Regis; OS Explorer 30 Exmouth and Sidmouth (GR 142078).

The Cistercians established an abbey near this village, on the southern slopes of the beautiful Blackdown Hills, in the 13th century. All that can be seen of it today, however, is the ruined gatehouse and a few bits of the walls, although a pretty little hamlet has grown up around the ruins, with a small, attractive church of its own.

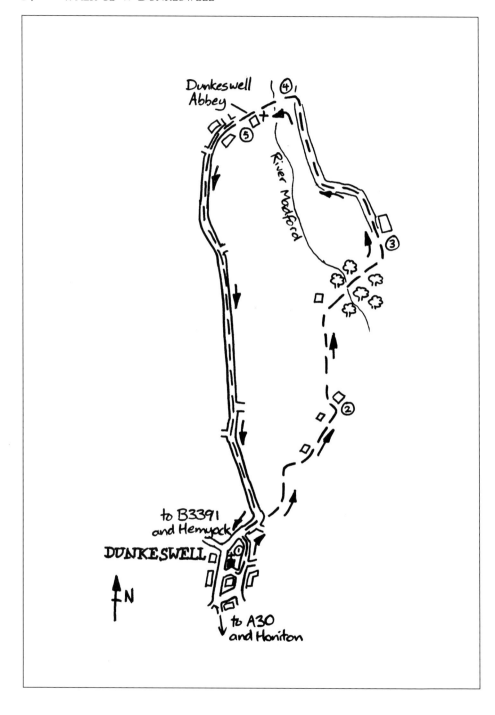

Dunkeswell itself lies 2 miles south of the abbey. It is a picturesque village of long, low farmhouses and thatched white cottages, all tucked away in an intricate network of little lanes surrounding the church. There is no main street as such (the road passes along the western edge of the village, overlooking the oldest part), and the only recognisable focal point is the church. Unusually, the pub is not in the centre of the village, but on the main road to the west. The village's layout makes exploring it an absolute delight – there are always treasures to be found hidden away down the side lanes.

The walk comprises mainly farm paths and quiet lanes, with some lovely views along the way. It takes you down through a pretty wood (with the chance to see some deer) to the river Madford and then along the side of the valley to the ruins of Dunkeswell Abbey before returning via an attractive lane, its hedges flower-filled in summer.

THE WALK
❶   The walk starts at the church, in the centre of Dunkeswell. If you have parked by the Royal Oak, go north (left as you leave the pub), take the first lane on the right, just beyond a pink cottage, and follow it

---

FOOD and DRINK

The Royal Oak Inn (telephone: 01404 891683), on the road past the village, has a wide-ranging menu, including salads, steaks and pies, as well as bar snacks such as jacket potatoes. There is also an animal sanctuary which children will love.

---

round to the left into the village. The church is on your left. Carry on round to the left, and at the T-junction turn right (signposted to Dunkeswell Abbey). The lane bends sharply to the left, and just beyond the bend is a public footpath sign on the right. Turn off here and go through a kissing gate. The path takes you along the top of a very steep bank, through some trees. After a short distance it goes left through another kissing gate and round to the right of a field, with a good view over the hedge on your right. You come out at a track; go right, and follow the track round a farm to a gate. Keep to the left of the field on the other side, with another very pretty view across the valley to your right. Go through another gate and to the left of the next field to a stile leading onto a track.

❷   Turn left and follow the track to the right round a farm. When the main track goes left, go straight on through a gate and then diagonally right across a field to a kissing gate, followed by a stile. Go straight across the next field to a gate. Keep to the right, alongside the fence, to a path. At the bottom go straight on past some farm buildings, through two gates and bear right down a track. This leads into a field. As it does so bear right again, keeping to the fence; you may be lucky enough to see the odd deer. Be careful along here as it can become very muddy. Cross a couple of iron bars at the bottom and make your way to the footbridge you will see ahead of you. Cross it and you will come to a set of steps up a bank, marked with a yellow waymark. Climb them and bear left along the top of the bank. At the end, follow the waymark straight ahead through the wood. The route here is clearly marked with regular way-marks. You soon come to another set of steps on your left; climb them, follow the path across a boardwalk and leave the wood via a stile. Follow the left-hand edge of the field round to a track.

❸ Turn left and you will be faced with two gates. Go through the left-hand one and follow the track through a farmyard and past a house. After a while the track becomes a surfaced lane. Continue for about ³/₄ mile.

❹ Look out for a black gate on your left, just before a house. There is a public footpath sign, but it is obscured from this direction by the hedge. Turn left here and bear left across the field to the far left-hand corner. Cross a footbridge and go diagonally left across the next field to a gate, then across the next field to another gate. Go left to cross a footbridge, then immediately right to follow a stream to a stile into a churchyard Go along the right-hand edge to a gap in the bank ahead onto a surfaced path. Some of the ruins of the abbey can be seen to your left, alongside the church. Turn right along the path to a gate into a

---

PLACES of INTEREST

At **Dunkeswell Air Centre**, just west of the village, children can enjoy a variety of rides and attractions with an aeronautical theme, or simply watch the aeroplanes and microlights. **Hembury**, 4 miles to the south-west, close to the A373, is one of the most impressive Iron Age hill forts in Devon. At **Hemyock**, 4¹/₂ miles to the north, there is a slightly more modern site, the ruins of a medieval castle. If you are interested in lace, then you should not miss **Allhallows Museum** in Honiton (5 miles), which has an exhibition of nearly 500 years of Honiton lace.

---

lane. The ruined gatehouse is on your left just before the gate.

❺ Follow the lane to a T-junction, and go straight on. The new road climbs steeply for a short distance before levelling off. It is a pretty lane, with flowers in the hedgerows on either side in summer, and it runs for about 1³/₄ miles back to Dunkeswell. On the edge of the village you come to a junction. Turn left to return to the church. To reach the Royal Oak, go straight on and at the T-junction turn left (signposted to Honiton).

STOCKLAND

Length : 6 miles

<table>
<tr><td>

Getting there: Stockland is signposted south off the A30 Honiton to Chard road just south-west of the junction with the A303. Follow the long, straight road for about 1³/₄ miles and then

</td><td>

turn left, again signposted to Stockland.

Parking: In the road. Please park with consideration, as some parts of the road are rather narrow.

</td><td>

Maps: OS Landranger 192 Exeter and Sidmouth or 193 Taunton and Lyme Regis (GR 244046).

</td></tr>
</table>

Strange though it may seem today, Stockland was once quite a major smuggling centre despite its distance from the coast; goods were brought up by river craft. For centuries, the parish was something of an anachronism: an island of Dorset territory completely surrounded by Devon, almost 10 miles from the rest of its county. In 1842, the situation was 'regularised' and it was incorporated into Devon.

It is a charming village, comprising mainly stone houses, many of which date back to the 15th and 16th centuries. The 14th-century church is set back a little

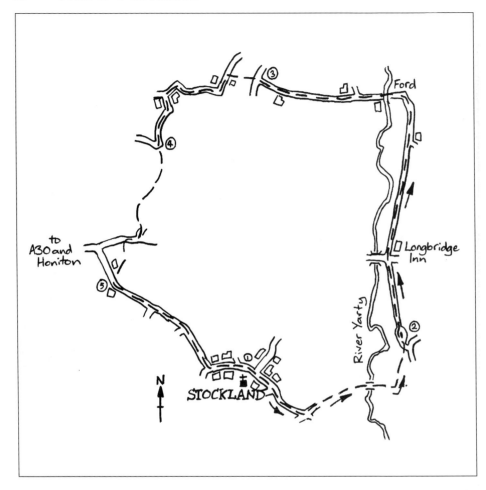

FOOD and DRINK

The village inn is the King's Arms (telephone: 01404 881361). It is a lovely pub and offers a very wide range of fare, from bar snacks and omelettes to steak and kidney pie and a full restaurant menu. If you would prefer to stop for refreshments along the way, the Longbridge Inn (telephone: 01404 881366) serves bar snacks, salads and steaks.

from the main road, but it is worth the detour to visit it, and the King's Arms is a gem of an inn.

The surrounding area is mainly agricultural, with some lovely old farmhouses scattered around the village, and our walk shows the rolling hills and lush farmland at their best. Most of the route follows quiet, pretty country lanes, lined with flowers in spring and summer, with some farm paths and tracks in between and one or two excellent viewpoints.

Luggs Farm near the village.

THE WALK

❶ Starting at the King's Arms, turn left (east), and at the road junction go straight on (signposted to the village hall, Membury and Axminster). Leave the village, passing the village hall on your left and a school on your right. When you see a road going off to the right, look out for a public footpath sign on the left. Go down a broad path and after a few yards you will see a stile on your right. Cross it and bear left along the edge of a field to a gap in the hedge ahead. Carry on along the left-hand side of the next field to a gateway, with a good view of the undulating farmland around you. Keep to the left of the next field to another gateway and then cross to a footbridge. Cross another field, still keeping to the left alongside a little stream to a footbridge across the river Yarty. Follow the right-hand edge of the next field to a stile and then cross some stepping stones over a rivulet slightly to your right. Once across the rivulet, turn left to reach a gate at the far end of the field. Follow a short track between hedges on the other side into a field. Keep to the right to another gate and cross a farmyard to a third gate leading into a lane.

❷ Turn left, and follow the lane for about ¹/₂ mile to a crossroads. Go straight on past the Longbridge Inn (or stop for refreshment if you feel so inclined), and after another ¹/₂ mile you will come to a junction; go left. There is another pretty view to the left over the valley of the river Yarty. After about 500 yards the lane turns sharply to the left and you come to a ford. If the river is high you can turn right off the lane just before the ford, following a footpath sign, and cross the river via a footbridge. In normal conditions, however, it is quite easy to cross at the ford. Go up the hill on the other side and at the junction go straight on.

❸ You come out at a T-junction. Cross the road ahead to a stile and go diagonally left across a field to another stile and a gate. Keep to the left of the next field to another stile which takes you out onto another lane; turn left. The lane goes to the right and to the left, and you get a good view over to the left. Shortly after the left-hand bend there is a fork; take the left-hand lane and follow it down a hill.

❹ As the lane takes a sharp turn to the right, round some dilapidated farm buildings, you will see a public footpath sign on your left. Follow it through a gate and across the field on the other side to a track. Do not go through the gate ahead but bear right up a field. Go through a gate at the end and bear left up the next field, with another very good view of the rolling

> **PLACES of INTEREST**
>
> At Honiton, about 5 miles away, is **Allhallows Museum**, with its superb exhibition of Honiton lace. **Cricket St Thomas**, which combines a wildlife park and gardens with a children's theme park that includes Noddy's Toytown, is about 8 miles away, on the other side of Chard. Also near Chard, 7¹/₂ miles from Stockland, is **Forde Abbey**, a stately home with a superb garden.

farmland to your left. As you come over the brow of the hill, you will see two gates in the left-hand hedge. Go through the second one and make your way up the next field towards the farm building on your right. Go round to the left of it to a gate, and go diagonally left across the next field to another gate, followed immediately by yet another. Go diagonally left across the next field to a stile by a house. Follow the drive up, crossing a cattle grid, to a lane; turn right. After about 200 yards the lane curves to the right. As it does so turn left across a stile marked with a public footpath sign. Go down the left-hand side of a field and you will come to a gate. Go right across the next field to a stile leading into a lane.

❺ Turn left and follow the lane for about ³/₄ mile to a T-junction. Turn left to return to the village.

NEWTON ST CYRES

Length : 6¹/₄ miles

Getting there: Newton St Cyres is on the A377, 4¹/₂ miles from Exeter and 2¹/₂ miles from Crediton.

Parking: There is a free public car park in the village, clearly marked from the main road.

Maps: OS Landranger 192 Exeter and Sidmouth (start and finish) and 191 Okehampton and North Dartmoor (middle section) (GR 879980).

Newton St Cyres straddles the A377, and to many travellers using that road it would seem to be little more than a pub and a few. But turn off the main road into the quiet lanes on either side and you will appreciate the delights of this pretty little farming village.

Just 4¹/₂ miles from Exeter, it could easily have become another dormitory village, surrounded by suburban development, but it has not. It retains the air of an unspoiled agricultural community, with its cob and thatch cottages clustered below the imposing 15th-century church.

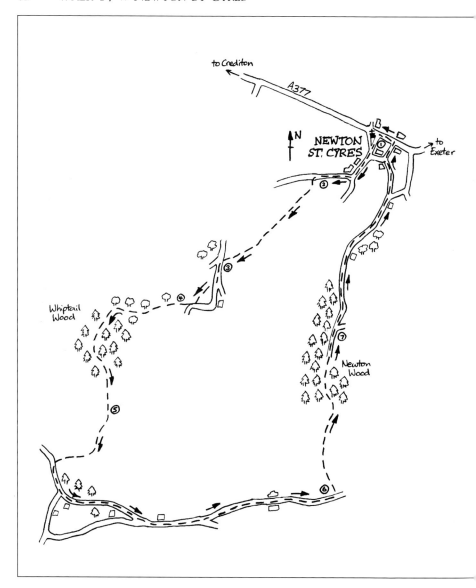

The village is surrounded by farms and woods, and they form the theme of this walk, along with pretty country lanes and excellent views. The terrain is generally undemanding, but there are one or two fairly steep climbs. There are also a few muddy stretches, so boots are recommended.

THE WALK

❶ From the car park, turn left, away from the main road. The lane goes alongside a small stream on the left and you soon leave the village. On the outskirts, you will find another lane going off to the left, marked with a 'no through road' sign. Ignore it and follow the main road round to the right as it climbs fairly steeply at first and then levels off.

❷   Near the top, you will find a public footpath sign pointing off to the left. Follow it through a gate, and go to the right of the field beyond. There are good views over hills and woods as you go. Cross a stile at the end of the field, and go diagonally right across the next field to another stile by a little stream. Cross this stile and then the stream, and go up the bank on the other side to another stile. Keep to the left of the next field. It is a long one, but eventually you come to a gate. Go through and keep to the right of the next field, and you will come to a gate leading into a lane. Be careful here, as it is muddy around the gate.

❸   Turn left into the lane and follow it down the hill. At the fork, go to the right, following the main lane. A few yards beyond the fork, you will see a public

---

FOOD and DRINK

The Crown and Sceptre (telephone: 01392 851278) is the only pub in the village, but you could not wish for anything better. It offers a wide range of meals, from doorstep sandwiches and imaginative ploughman's lunches (try their Lincolnshire sausage ploughman's) to traditional dishes such as fried scampi and daily specials like freshly baked turkey and mushroom pie. It also has a delightful riverside patio. If you prefer to picnic, the village shop can supply the wherewithal.

---

footpath sign pointing half right up a bank behind some trees. Follow this. Cross a stile and keep to the right of the field on the other side. You will come to two stiles on your right; ignore the first and cross the second, which is marked with a yellow arrow. This leads you into a wood. Follow the path down the hill to the left until you come to another lane. Go right and follow the lane as it climbs to the left, between some gateposts.

❹   At the top, just as the lane curves to the left again, go right, following the public footpath sign. The path goes down into Whiptail Wood, and then goes left to contour round the hill. The path through this stretch of woods is very clear, and where there is any chance of your missing the route, there are the yellow waymarks to guide you. About 600 yards after leaving the lane, you go through a gate and the path starts to curve to the left, climbing as it does so. You will come across several tracks on this stretch, but your route is clearly marked by yellow waymarks, and it is very easy to find your way. You will eventually leave the deciduous wood and enter a dense conifer plantation, climbing again as you do so.

❺   The path finally leads you to the edge of the wood, where you will find a gate on your right, with a yellow waymark on the gatepost. Go through the gate onto a grassy track, which leads into a long field. Keep to the right. After about 300 yards, you will find another grassy track on your right, between two hedges. Follow that. Some way along it you will come to a wire barrier across the track. It opens like a gate, so go through it, and a few yards further on you will come to a proper gate leading into a lane. Turn left. After about 300 yards, there is a junction. Turn left to re-enter the woods (signposted to Whitestone church and Exeter). At the next junction, turn left again (signposted to Whitestone church and Exeter again). There is a superb view to the right, across to the river Exe and South Devon. After another $1/2$ mile there is another junction. Go left here (signposted to Rowhorne). Continue for about $1/2$ mile, passing Rowhorne Farm on the left and West Rowhorne Farm on the right.

❻ About 300 yards beyond the farms, turn sharp left off the road, following a public bridleway sign. It can be very muddy along here, but you soon come to a gate, and the field beyond is drier. Keep to the left around the top of the field to another gate, and along a short track to a third gate. Keep to the right of the next field to another gate, which leads into Newton Wood. At the track junction a short distance into the wood, turn right. The track itself tends to be muddy at first, but there is enough room to walk on the bank

---

PLACES of INTEREST

Exeter is only $4^{1}/_{2}$ miles away, and there is a great deal to interest the visitor there, including the cathedral, several museums, the ancient city walls and underground passages. Slightly further afield (about 9 miles to the east) is **Killerton House**, a National Trust property renowned for its costume collection.

---

beside it, and so avoid the worst of the mud. At the next track junction, go straight on. You now have the wood on your left, and a hedge on your right. The track leads to a lane. Go straight on along the lane, still with the wood on your left and a hedge on your right. As you come over the brow of the hill and leave the wood behind you, yet another lovely view across the farms and woods opens up ahead.

❼ About $3/4$ mile after joining the lane, you come to a fork. Go left, following the road marked 'not suitable for long vehicles'. It takes you down into Newton St Cyres, between some beautiful thatched cottages, to join the A377 opposite the Crown and Sceptre. Turn left, and then left again to return to the car park.

STICKLEPATH

Length : 3¹/₂ miles

Getting there: The village is near Okehampton, just south of the A30 from Exeter to Cornwall, and is clearly signposted from both directions.	Parking: In the road through the village.	Maps: OS Landranger 191 Okehampton and North Dartmoor; OS Outdoor Leisure 28 Dartmoor (GR 641941).

Sticklepath is a one-street village on the northern edge of Dartmoor comprising a mixture of stone and slate and cob and thatch houses. It has 24 listed buildings. The Taw River Inn, on the northern side of the street, is a traditional Devon long-house, and was once the manor house.

John Wesley preached in the village in 1743, and it retains its strong Methodist tradition. It is also home to Finch Foundry, a 19th-century water-powered forge which is still in working order. It is owned by the National Trust and there are regular demonstrations.

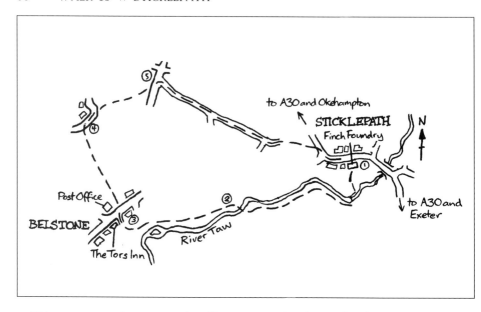

This area was the setting for Henry Williamson's classic *Tarka the Otter* – indeed, the river Taw, where much of the action takes place, skirts the southern edge of Sticklepath. The walk follows a short stretch of the Tarka Trail (a route which takes in many of the places referred to in the book) alongside the river and through some lovely woodland to the pretty neighbouring village of Belstone. It then leaves the river and crosses farmland to the very edge of the Dartmoor National Park before returning to Sticklepath along farm tracks, with some excellent views of both the moor and the surrounding farms and woods.

THE WALK

❶   Start at Finch Foundry in the centre of the village. Go through the archway into the garden at the rear, and follow the drive round to the right towards the car park. Just before you reach it, turn left along a path. At the end bear left, following the sign pointing to the Two Museums Walk, and go down to the river Taw. Follow the river upstream for a short distance until you come to a footbridge. Cross it and turn right along a track, still following the sign for the Two Museums Walk. Go through a gate and turn right (signposted to Skaigh Woods and Skaigh). This path takes you

---

FOOD and DRINK

The two pubs in Sticklepath are both excellent in their own ways. The Devonshire Inn (telephone: 01837 840628) has retained its traditional atmosphere, but only serves sandwiches and pasties. The Taw River Inn (telephone: 01837 840377) has been somewhat modernised, but has a more extensive menu, ranging from bar snacks to a variety of main meals. There is also a National Trust tearoom at Finch Foundry, and if you want a break just under halfway through the walk, try the Tors Inn at Belstone. The post office in Sticklepath sells pasties and other picnic ingredients.

The entrance to Finch Foundry.

through a lovely deciduous wood alongside the river. After a while you cross a stile. This is a beautiful stretch, with a mass of rhododendrons on one side and the river chattering and tumbling over the rocks on the other. You eventually come to a gate and a footbridge. Cross over and make your way up to a track.

❷   Turn left (signposted to Belstone and the moor). The track takes you a little away from the river, although you can still see it through the trees on your left. It narrows to a path and curves away from the river, and the trees thin out. The path continues through the bracken and then climbs somewhat steeply to the right out of the valley. As you get to the top, you get a good view across to the moor on the left. You eventually come out at a field on the edge of Belstone; cross it to a road and turn right into the village, passing the Tors Inn as you go.

❸   At the end of the road, by the post office, turn right and after a few yards, just beyond a bench, you will see a public footpath sign on the left, pointing to Higher Priestacott. Turn left and go through two gates into a field. Keep to the right and cross a bank at the end into another field. Keep to the right again to reach a gateway. Go through and keep left to a stile. Go diagonally right across the next field to a double stile. You then cross a very short field to three stiles in quick succession and cross the next field to yet another stile. Follow the edge of the next field to a final stile, with a very good view ahead of you as you go. Keep to the left of the next field to a gate into the garden of a house.

❹ Follow the drive past the house to a lane and turn right. The road twists to the left, to the right and to the left again, and just after its second left-hand bend you will see a public footpath sign on the right, pointing to Tongue End. Cross a stile into a field and go straight across to a gate in the middle of the bank ahead. Cross the next field to a gap in the bank and go half left across the next field to two gates alongside a pumping station. Although the public footpath sign is at the left-hand of the two gates, that is fairly firmly tied closed, so it is best to use the right-hand one. This leads you into a lane; turn left.

❺ About 100 yards along the lane you will come to a cattle grid, with a gate on the

---

PLACES of INTEREST

Finch Foundry, in the village, is worth a visit. And just 4 miles away, in Okehampton, is the **Museum of Dartmoor Life**, with reconstructions and exhibitions of the heritage of the moor, as well as the ruins of **Okehampton Castle**, a Norman castle now in the hands of English Heritage.

---

right just before it. Turn right through the gate onto a track (signposted to Skaigh and Sticklepath). As you follow this track you get another fine view over undulating farmland on your left, and a little later across to the moor on your right. You cross a cattle grid, with a track going off to the right; ignore it, and the next one (signposted to Skaigh), and carry straight on. The track leads you to a gate; go through and follow the path on the other side. As it emerges into the open, you get an excellent view ahead, with Sticklepath nestling below you. The path comes out at a house; go right to follow a track steeply downhill. At the bottom, cross a lane to the pavement on the other side, and follow the main road back into the village.

DREWSTEIGNTON

Length : 5 miles

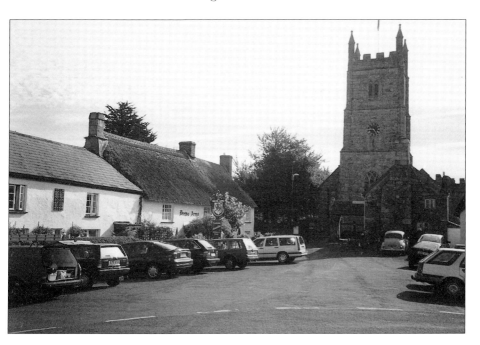

Getting there:
Drewsteignton lies about 1¹/₂ miles east of the A382 Moretonhampstead to Okehampton road and 1¹/₂ miles south of the A30 between Exeter and Okehampton, and is signposted from both directions.

Parking: In the village square, next to the church.

Maps: OS Landranger 191 Okehampton and North Dartmoor; OS Outdoor Leisure 28 Dartmoor (GR 736908).

Drewsteignton derives its name from a Norman knight, Drogo de Teigne, after whom the nearby Castle Drogo was also named. Despite its name – and its appearance – however, the 'castle' is in fact an early 20th-century country house.

The village itself is a picturesque collection of thatched and slate-roofed houses and cottages above the Teign Gorge. The focal point is the central square, with the church at one end. The church dates mainly from the 15th and 16th centuries,

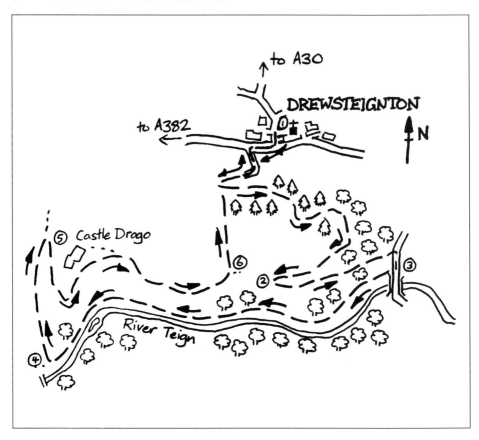

but the pews, with their carved ends, show the 20th-century influence of the Drewes of Castle Drogo. Another landmark of the village is the Drewe Arms, close by the church. Dating back to the 17th century, it still retains much of its original layout and character. Its main claim to fame is that it has had the longest-serving landlady in the country. Mabel Mudge ('Aunty' to her regulars) held the licence from 1919 to 1994 when, well into her nineties, she finally retired. She has since died.

The Teign Gorge is one of the most spectacular areas in Devon, and this walk takes you through the woods along the bottom of the valley and then back along the top of the gorge, with magnificent views up the river to the moors. If you are so minded, there is also an opportunity to visit Castle Drogo along the way.

THE WALK

❶ Turn left out of the village square and then right (signposted to Whiddon Down, Chagford and Moretonhampstead). After about 100 yards, near the edge of the village, you will see a track leading off to the left, signposted to the Hunter's Path, Fingle Bridge and the road near Castle Drogo. Follow it down a hill and to the

The delightful Angler's Rest at Fingle Bridge.

right. At the junction at the bottom go left (signposted to Fingle Bridge). This track leads into a quiet wood. When the track forks go right (signposted to the Hunter's Path and Castle Drogo) to climb up above the valley. It is a long but fairly easy climb. At the top fork left (signposted to the Hunter's Path again). You are now in a conifer plantation and the track contours round the hill, first right, then left, then right again, narrowing to a path as it does so. As you go round the path clings to the side of the hill, with the wood stretching steeply down to the River Teign to your left. You eventually leave the wood and get a superb view up the gorge to Castle Drogo and the moors beyond.

❷ When you come to a path junction, turn sharp left, almost back on yourself (signposted to Fingle Bridge). This stretch is a picture in late summer, with the yellow of the gorse and the purple of the heather colouring the slopes around you. You re-enter the wood and begin to descend. After about 600 yards the path curves to the left and goes down to a road. Turn sharp right and follow the road to Fingle Bridge.

❸ Just before the bridge, turn right through a kissing gate (signposted as the Fisherman's Path to Dogmarsh Bridge, Chagford and the road near Castle Drogo). The path initially takes you above the river

FOOD and DRINK

You have a choice of two pubs on this walk, both of which I can highly recommend. The Drewe Arms in Drewsteignton itself (telephone: 01647 281224) is full of atmosphere and character and serves a range of delicious home-made fare, including fesh sandwiches, ploughman's lunches made with local cheeses and chutneys and main dishes such as farmhouse pie and cheese and broccoli flan. The Angler's Rest at Fingle Bridge (telephone: 01647 281287), which you pass along the way, has a lovely situation right by the river, and serves a selection of snacks and sandwiches, with main courses which include such delights as lamb and apricot pie and smoked fish platter. The Old Inn Restaurant in Drewsteignton serves coffees, teas and light lunches, and the village post office sells pasties and sandwiches. There is also a National Trust restaurant at Castle Drogo.

and then goes down to the bank. This is a gorgeous stretch, with plenty of places where you can stop and picnic by the river. The path forks from time to time. It is usually best to keep to the more clearly defined route furthest from the river to avoid further erosion of the bank, which is already crumbling badly in places. Continue for about $1^1/_2$ miles of lovely riverside.

❹   When you come to a rather spectacular weir followed by a footbridge turn right to leave the river, just after the bridge.

PLACES of INTEREST

Castle Drogo, in the immediate vicinity, and 8 miles away, just beyond Moretonhampstead, the **Miniature Pony Centre** which, as its name suggests, specialises in miniature ponies, but which also has many other farm animals that children can handle and cuddle.

Go through a gateway onto a track, climbing gently as you go. You join another track and bear right, following the public footpath sign. Through the trees on your right you can just see the top of Castle Drogo on its promontory. The track ends at a lane, where you bear right again, continuing for another 300 yards or so.

❺   Follow a sign pointing sharp right to the Hunter's Path, and go through a gate onto a track. The granite bulk of Castle Drogo looms above you on the left and you get a good view ahead over a patchwork of farms and woods. As you go round the hill you get another lovely view down the gorse, heather and bracken-clad slopes of the Teign Gorge.

You will come to a path off to the left signposted to Castle Drogo. Turn up here if you want to visit the castle; otherwise continue straight on. You will pass another path to Castle Drogo, and a few hundred yards after that another path to the left, this time signposted to Drewsteignton and Piddledown.

❻   Turn off here and climb to a stile. Keep to the left of the field beyond. Cross a stile into another field and keep to the left of that to go down to another stile into a wood. Follow the path steeply down on the other side and at the junction at the bottom of the hill go straight on. You are now on the track you came out on, so follow it back up to the road and turn right to return to Drewsteignton.

DUNSFORD

Length : 4¹/₂ miles

Getting there: Dunsford lies just north of the B3212 Exeter to Moretonhampstead road, and is clearly signposted from each direction.	Parking: In the village streets.	Map: OS Landranger 191 Okehampton and North Dartmoor (GR 813891).

This lovely little village originated as a simple river crossing, where cattle coming down from their summer pastures crossed the Teign – hence the name ('dunn' means cattle). Most of the houses are of cob and many are still thatched, and they make a particularly beautiful picture in the sum-

mer when they are wreathed in flowers growing from hanging baskets, window boxes and trellises.

The attractive church dates from the 15th century, but the village pub, the Royal Oak, is much more modern – a red-brick Victorian building which replaced the

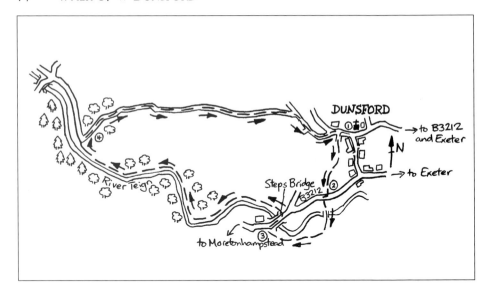

earlier inn when it was destroyed by fire. It is a delightful place inside – comfortable and welcoming – but the exterior is somewhat out of keeping with the traditional style of the rest of the village.

FOOD and DRINK

There are two pubs to choose from, both with their own attractions. Despite its outward appearance, the Royal Oak in Dunsford itself (telephone: 01647 252256) has a lot of atmosphere and is a friendly place. Its menu ranges from potato wedges and soup and rolls to steaks and scampi. The Steps Bridge Inn at Steps Bridge (telephone: 01647 252313) has the advantage of being right on the river, with lovely views over the water. It does teas and coffees as well as a range of meals, including sandwiches, ploughman's lunches and daily specials such as seafood bake. The post office in Dunsford will be able to supply you with the wherewithal if you want to picnic by the river, and behind it is a walled tea garden offering sandwiches, pies and pasties in addition to tea and coffee.

Much of the woodland in the area is owned by the National Trust and managed as a nature reserve, and this walk takes you along some of the prettiest routes through it. You amble along the riverside through woods carpeted with wild flowers (especially in the spring), before returning along a quiet country lane flanked by hedgerows filled with more flowers.

THE WALK

❶ Starting at the church, go west (right as you come out of the churchyard), past the pub, the village hall and the school. Just beyond the school is a small road on the left. Turn down it and at the end you will find a narrow path running to the left of a house (signposted to the B3212 near the mill). Follow it to a stile and then go straight on to the corner of a hedge, which is marked by a yellow-topped post. Go round the hedge, through a gap in a fence on the right and then left to cut across a field, following the yellow waymarks painted

The river Teign at Steps Bridge.

on the trees. Near the end of the field you will see a stile on your left; cross it and turn right, following the hedge on your right. When the hedge swings away to the right, go straight on to a gate leading onto a road. Go through and turn right.

❷ Just beyond the Dunsford Mills Country Hotel turn left, following the public footpath sign to Bridford Wood. This takes you down to the river and across some stepping stones – a child's paradise. On the other side there is a path across some open ground to a surfaced track. Turn right (signposted to Steps Bridge). After a few yards you come to a gateway leading to a house. Turn left and follow the path up into the wood. This is a beautiful stretch, full of flowers and birdlife. The path takes you above the river, which you can see flowing along in a succession of rapids and quiet pools down on your right.

❸ The path comes out at a road just opposite the Steps Bridge Inn. Turn right and follow the road across the bridge. Immediately on the other side, turn left along a bridlepath (signposted to the county road near Clifford Bridge). You pass a weir and enter another pretty wood, again with a wealth of birdlife all around. This stretch is particularly renowned for its spring flowers. At the notice board giving information about Dunsford Wood, the path divides. Take the right fork, following the bridlepath sign. This takes you away from the river, but you soon rejoin it and continue along the bank. There are some lovely spots along here where you can stop for a picnic. The path forks again from time to time, and each time it does so you

should follow the bridlepath sign away from the river; the diversion is usually to avoid further erosion of the riverbank.

❹ After following the woodland path for 1½ miles, you come to a footbridge and then a lane. Turn right and follow the lane as it climbs gently through the wood and then leaves it. It continues to climb in a long, steady ascent between high hedges filled with wild flowers in season. After about ¾ mile it stops climbing and begins to descend, and as it does so, you get a very good view across the farmland ahead of you. At the first junction, follow the main road round to the right (signposted to Dunsford) and at the next carry straight on into the village.

NORTH BOVEY

Length : 4¹/₂ miles

Getting there: North Bovey can only be reached via narrow country lanes. The best approaches are from Moretonhampstead and Bovey Tracey. From Moretonhampstead, take the B3212 Princetown road and turn off left, following the signs to North Bovey. From Bovey Tracey, take the road to Manaton and then again follow the signs to North Bovey.

Parking: There is a free car park opposite the church, on the south side of the village. Alternatively, one can park around the village green.

Maps: OS Landranger 191 Okehampton and North Dartmoor; OS Outdoor Leisure 28 Dartmoor (GR 739838).

The age of this picturesque, unspoilt little village is attested by the ancient oaks on the green, the 13th-century church and the pub, the Ring of Bells, which was built in 1248 to house the masons building the church. The green is the focal point, and is surrounded by pretty thatched cottages, some built of the local granite, some of whitewashed cob. The pub is set back a little on one side and the church on the

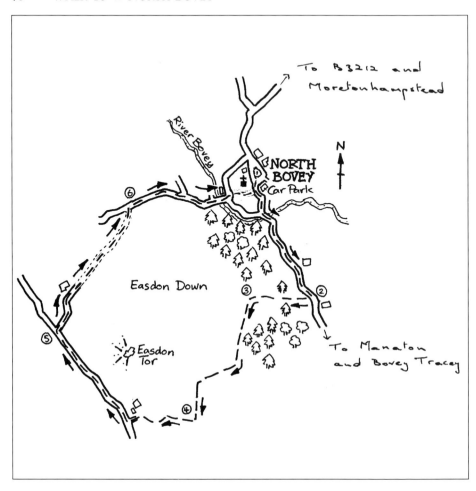

other, and the tranquil scene does not appear to have changed much for several centuries – even the village pump remains in the centre of the green.

The village lies towards the eastern edge of Dartmoor, and the surrounding country-side consequently comprises an interesting mix of lush green farm fields and barren moorland. This walk takes in a bit of both, with a delightful stretch of woodland thrown in for good measure. And some of the views you will enjoy along the way are quite magnificent. Apart from the moor-land terrain of Easdon Down and the wood that leads up to it, the route follows easy lanes, flower-lined in summer, and farm tracks for virtually its whole length.

THE WALK

❶   Head south from the village green (or left out of the car park, depending on where you start). Follow the lane down to cross the river, pass Aller Farm and Aller Mill on your left and climb the hill beyond;

The village pump stands proudly on the green.

it is a steep but mercifully short ascent.

❷   Near the top you will pass some houses on your right, and just beyond, as the lane levels off, you will find a path leading sharp right through a gate; there is a public

bridlepath sign pointing to Barracott via Easdon, but it is not very clear as it is set back some way from the road. A grassy track leads you between banks of wild flowers in season, to pass along the edge of a conifer plantation. Go through another gate and bear right to follow a well-worn path up the hill. After a short distance you will join a broad track; bear right, following the path sign. This area is a mass of foxgloves in summer. When you come to a surfaced track, go straight across, still following the path sign. Go through another gate and follow the path up through the trees on the other side, with a wall on your right. Take care, as it can become muddy after rain.

FOOD and DRINK

The lovely old Ring of Bells (telephone: 01647 440375) is a superb example of a traditional Dartmoor inn, with its thatched roof and whitewashed walls and an atmosphere to match. It has a wide-ranging menu: jacket potatoes and ploughman's lunches at one end of the scale and pork Devonshire and home-made steak and kidney pie at the other. There are also a number of vegetarian and fish dishes.

❸   When the wall curves right, keep to the path that leads straight up the hill to Easdon Down. Towards the top it forks; take the left-hand fork, heading for the corner of a plantation. As you go, look over to your left for a lovely view across the Bovey valley to Lustleigh Cleave. When you come to a wall, go right to follow it round and then take the path which bears a little away from it. You now get another excellent view, not only to the left but also ahead, with the unmistakable double hump of Haytor on the horizon. When you come to another wall, go straight on, keeping the wall on your left and the rocks of Easdon Tor on your right. At the next corner, turn left and follow the wall down to a track.

❹   Turn right and follow the track alongside another wall. After about 300 yards, the track curves left through a gate and down between two walls to a group of houses. Go left to circumnavigate them and you will come out on a surfaced lane. At the T-junction turn right onto another flower-filled lane, with good views ahead and to the left. Continue for about $1/2$ mile.

❺   Turn right up a lane marked with a 'no through road' sign. There is a short climb and then the lane twists to the left, the right and the left again to a farm. Go straight on through the farm to another track between walls. Soon you will see the gentle slopes of Easdon Down over the wall on your right, and then the track begins to descend. Continue for just over $1/2$ mile.

❻   When the track comes out onto a lane, turn right. At the next junction go

PLACES of INTEREST

Just 1$1/2$ miles north-west of North Bovey, on the Moretonhampstead to Princetown road, is the **Miniature Pony Centre**, with a number of farmyard attractions for children. About 3 miles in the other direction, near Manaton, **Becky Falls** has nature trails, a lovely waterfall and a pets' corner, and another 4 miles beyond that lies Bovey Tracey, which offers a number of attractions: the **Riverside Centre**, headquarters of the Devon Guild of Craftsmen; the **Cardew Teapottery**, where you can see teapots being made; and the **House of Marbles**, which has demonstrations of glassblowing.

straight on (signposted to North Bovey). The lane descends steeply to cross the river Bovey and then bends to the left. As it does so, you should go straight on up to a path (signposted to North Bovey village and church). At the gate into the churchyard at the top, turn right to go round it, or go through the gate if you want to explore the church. At the road, go straight across to the car park or turn left to reach the village green.

WALK 19

TRUSHAM

Length : 4¹/₂ miles

Getting there: Turn east off the B3193 Teign valley road between Chudleigh and Christow.	**Parking:** There are a few parking places in the centre of the village, just above the children's playground. If those are full, you may be able to find a space alongside the road through the village.	**Maps:** OS Landranger 191 Okehampton and North Dartmoor; OS Explorer 31 Torquay and Dawlish (GR 854821).

There is a string of pretty villages and hamlets running up the Teign valley and the coombes that lead off it, but none is prettier than Trusham. Its whitewashed cottages and narrow lanes make it a delight to wander through. It presents an attrac- tive and sympathetic mixture of architec- tural styles and periods, from the traditional to the modern – the older houses mainly along the valley floor and the newer ones climbing the hills on either side.

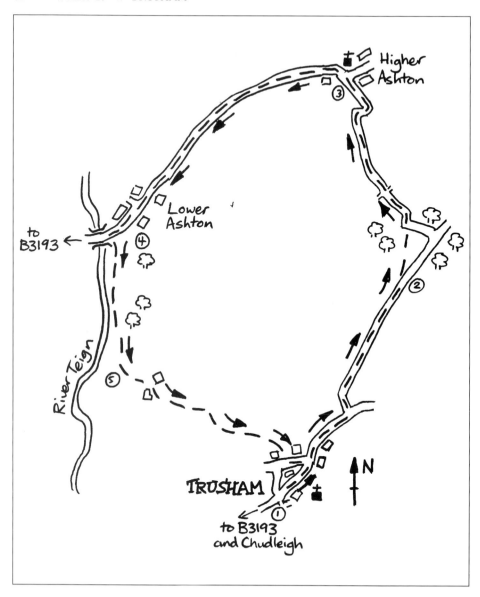

A little way up the valley, and linked with Trusham by narrow, often flower-filled lanes, are the equally delightful twin hamlets of Higher and Lower Ashton. The walk takes you along the lanes to visit them and then brings you back to Trusham alongside the river Teign and over farm fields. And as if that were not enough, there are also some lovely views to enjoy along the way.

THE WALK

❶ Follow the main road north-east through the village, passing the Cridford Inn on the left and then climbing out into open country. At the junction about 1/4 mile out of the village, follow the main road round to the left (signposted to Ashton and Exeter). You continue to climb up a pretty lane past some farms, with good views across to Haldon Forest on the right. It is quite a long climb, but a fairly easy one. You pass a house called Cherry Orchard on your right, and about 200 yards beyond it you will see a public footpath sign in the hedge on your right, but pointing left.

❷ Turn left here, through a gate, and bear right in the field beyond, more or less parallel to the lane. There is a superb view to the left across the Teign valley to the woods beyond. At the end of the field there is a stile; cross it and bear left to skirt round to the right of a copse. Cross another stile to enter the copse and follow the path down a hill. At the bottom bear right to follow the line of a bank to yet another stile leading to a lane. Go straight on down the lane, passing the pretty Embercombe Cottage as you go, and as you come over the

---

FOOD and DRINK

The Cridford Inn (telephone: 01626 853694) is a lovely old pub, where you can be sure of a warm welcome. It offers a range of dishes, from soups and salads to farmhouse grills and fish and vegetarian dishes, but not things like sandwiches or ploughman's lunches. If you want a break along the way, you might like to try the Manor Inn at Lower Ashton (telephone: 01647 252304), which also has a wide-ranging menu.

---

brow of the hill you get another good view up ahead. You continue down between hedges, flower-filled in season, past more attractive thatched houses, to Higher Ashton.

❸ At the junction go straight on (signposted to Lower Ashton and Christow). You cross a stream and follow the lane for about 3/4 mile, past Ashton Manor, to Lower Ashton. Despite its small size, this picturesque hamlet of attractive whitewashed cottages boasts both a pub (the Manor Inn) and a village shop. Go straight through it and out the other side.

❹ About 150 yards beyond the Manor Inn, as the lane bends to the right, turn left up a narrow track. This leads to a field which is used as a campsite in summer. Here you have a choice. There is a delightful path round to the right of the field, which takes you along the tree-lined river bank with the Teign gliding gently along beside you. But it is not much used towards the end and so tends to become rather overgrown. Last time I walked along it, I had to fight my way through brambles and nettles for a stretch of about 20 yards or so. The alternative is to follow the track into the field and across it; both routes come out at the same point, on a broad track (which is the line of a disused railway). Follow this until your way is blocked by a gate.

❺ At the gate turn left off the track, along a path. You will find a gate ahead of you, marked 'private'. Turn right to follow a path to a gate (which was hardly visible when I last walked this route because of the bindweed entwining it). Cross the gate and the (equally overgrown) footbridge beyond it to a field. Bear left up the field, following the broad, grassy track which goes round slightly to the right of the hill, rather than the narrow path which goes straight up. Go through a gap in the bank and follow the track alongside another bank on the left. You get a magnificent view back across the valley as you go.

Go through a gate and across a farmyard, with holiday cottages on your left, and follow the track on the other side. Go through a gap in the next hedge and continue to follow the track along the right-hand side of the next field. About 150 yards after going through the hedge you will find a stile on your right, marked with a yellow arrow. Cross it and go along the right-hand side of a field. You get another good view ahead of you to complement the excellent one you continue to enjoy across the valley on the left. At the end of the field, cross some rather makeshift fencing onto a muddy track between hedges. Turn left, and when the hedge on your right ends you will find another stile marked with a yellow arrow.

PLACES of INTEREST

Canonteign Falls, said to be the highest in England, are about $2^1/_2$ miles to the west, and in addition to the falls themselves, there is a wildlife park and children's play areas. The **Wheel Craft Centre** at Chudleigh (4 miles) offers the opportunity to see craftspeople at work, while another mile further on is **Ugbrooke House**, a very interesting historic house. Bovey Tracey is also only 4 miles away, and there you can visit the **Riverside Centre** (the headquarters of the Devon Guild of Craftsmen) and a number of other attractions, including the **House of Marbles**, where you can see glassblowers at work, and **Cardew Teapottery**, which has demonstrations of teapots being made.

Cross it and follow the right-hand hedge alongside the field. You can now see Trusham ahead of you. At the end of the field, follow the hedge round to your left, and in the far corner you will find another stile. Follow the path on the other side down the hill to yet another stile. Beyond that, the path takes you between some cottages to a small footbridge. Turn left up the lane on the other side and at the junction turn sharp right to return to the parking area.

KENTON
Length : 7½ miles

| Getting there: The village is on the A379 between Exeter and Dawlish. | Parking: There is a free public car park just off the main road, near the church. | Map: OS Landranger 192 Exeter and Sidmouth (GR 958832). |

Kenton was once a thriving centre; ships used to sail up the river Kenn bringing wine and spirits and taking the local salt for export. Today it is a pretty little backwater which, despite being on quite a major holiday route, retains its tranquil charm. A major fire destroyed half the buildings in the village in 1856, and it now presents a pleasant blend of traditional, Victorian and modern homes.

The church dates from the 14th century, and is worth a visit. The rood screen has panels depicting 40 saints and prophets, and the pulpit is said to have been made from a single oak.

This undemanding ramble takes you past Powderham Castle, the stately 15th-century home of the Earls of Devon, to the beautiful lower Exe, internationally re-nowned for its birdlife. You then follow

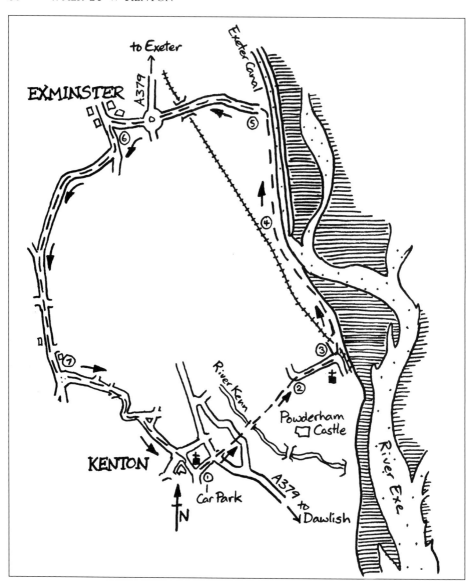

the peaceful Exeter Canal to Exminster and return via quiet lanes.

THE WALK

❶ Go out of the car park and turn right onto the A379, then almost immediately left opposite the Dolphin Inn, following the public footpath sign. You go through a gate and alongside a stream to another gate. Cross the road on the other side, and follow the path into open countryside. Cross the river Kenn via a footbridge, and then go

The path near Kenton.

FOOD and DRINK

Kenton's two pubs stand almost opposite each other on the main road, and both offer good fare. The Dolphin Inn (telephone: 01626 891371) has snacks and sandwiches as well as a range of main courses, including their Dolphin Grill for those with a hearty appetite. Vegetarians are also well catered for. The Devon Arms (telephone: 01626 890213) has a traditional pub menu, with main courses comprising mainly steaks, sausages and so on. The village shop has pasties and other picnic ingredients. If you would prefer to stop along the way, the Turf Hotel, at the junction of the river Exe and the Exeter Canal (telephone: 01392 833128) is a good place, although it only offers lunches, and at Exminster, on the return leg, you will find the Swan Inn and the Royal Oak.

through a gate and across a track. The path leads up the hill on the other side of the track. To the right lie the grounds of Powderham Castle. Soon you will be able to see the castle itself to your right, with a very good view across to the estuary beyond. The area on your immediate right is the castle's deer park, and you should see a large herd grazing nearby.

❷ At the top of the hill, cross a stile into a field. Keep to the right of the field, with views of the Exe up ahead, and follow the fence as it curves right. Look out for pheasants along here. Go through a kissing gate to a green. Cross it to join a road, and follow it straight ahead to a church.

❸   Bear left with the road to go around the church, and just as the road bends to the right, turn left along a path, following the public footpath sign. This path takes you alongside a railway line, then turns right to cross it. Cross carefully, then turn left alongside the river. This area, all the way down to Dawlish Warren, is an internationally important site for waterfowl and wading birds, and some very large flocks can be seen at times. About $1\frac{1}{4}$ miles after crossing the railway line, the path goes right, through a kissing gate, to the point where the Exeter Canal enters the Exe.

❹   Turn left, past the lock, and follow the path which runs along the edge of the canal, with the sights and sounds of this tranquil stretch of water for company. Continue for about $3/4$ mile.

❺   When you reach a parking area on the left, go through it and follow the track beyond, which after a while becomes a surfaced lane. After about $1/2$ mile you cross the railway line via a bridge, and then come to a roundabout at the A379. Go straight across into Exminster.

❻   You pass a new housing estate and then, as the road curves to the right, turn left up Exminster Hill. There is a fairly long but not too steep climb out of the village, and then, just over the brow of the hill, you fork right into a narrow lane. There are pleasant views over farmland and woods as

---

PLACES of INTEREST

Powderham Castle, whose grounds you pass on the walk, is open on summer afternoons. At Starcross, $1\frac{1}{2}$ miles away, is the **Brunel Atmospheric Railway**, a historic building erected by I. K. Brunel which incorporates his atmospheric railway and other scientific exhibits, while 3 miles beyond that is the lovely nature reserve of **Dawlish Warren**, which is noted for its waterfowl. And only 6 miles away in the other direction is the city of **Exeter**, with its cathedral, museums and historic city centre.

---

you go, with the River Exe to your left. After about $3/4$ mile you will come to some woodland on your left, and soon after that you join another lane. Turn left (signposted to Kenton). It is a pretty lane, almost devoid of traffic, with high banks on either side and pheasants darting in and out of the woods on the left. At the crossroads beyond the woods, go straight on (signposted to Mamhead). Do not follow the road to the left, even though it is signposted to Kenton, as it will take you to the A379, which is very busy and unpleasant to walk along.

❼   About $1/2$ mile beyond the crossroads, take the lane that leads off to the left. You will pass a pig farm on the right and then Chiverstone Farm on the left. At the next fork, bear right. After a while you will see the tower of Kenton church ahead. At the main road, go left and then bear right into the village. Follow the road round the church and you will see the car park on the right.

WALK 21

OTTERTON

Length : 5¹/₄ miles

Getting there: The village is just east of the B3178 Newton Poppleford to Budleigh Salterton road.	**Parking:** Alongside the green or further along the main street of the village.	**Maps:** OS Landranger 192 Exeter and Sidmouth; OS Explorer 30 Exmouth and Sidmouth (GR 082852).

Otterton is a picture-postcard Devon village of cob and thatch cottages and traditional cross-passage farmhouses, with a stream running down its main street and a medieval mill at one end. It is no museum piece, however, but a working community with a history dating back to Saxon times.

Until the mid-15th century, it was a thriving fishing village. Given its position and the present state of the river Otter this may seem surprising, but until that time the estuary stretched all the way up to the village and there was easy access to the sea. The other mainstay of the economy was milling. William the Conqueror granted the village to the monks of Mont St Michel, who built a priory where the

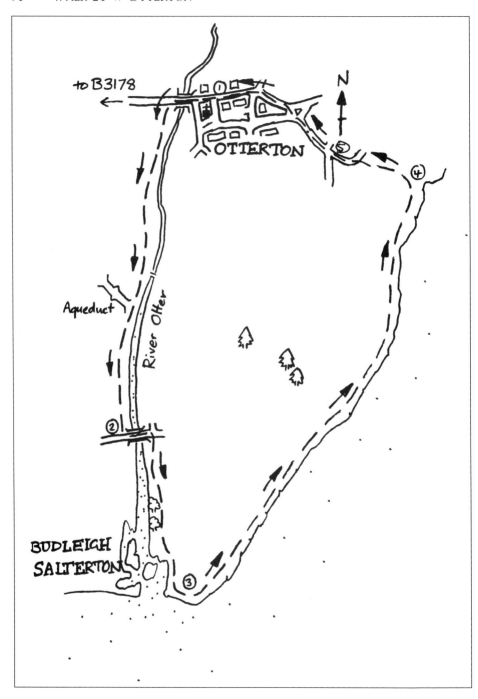

Otterton Mill.

present church is and a mill on the river. Although nothing remains of the original mill, the medieval buildings which you see on the site today give some idea of its

---

FOOD and DRINK

The village pub, the King's Arms (telephone: 01395 568416) has a very diverse menu, offering a variety of bar snacks and daily specials which range from steaks to fish, chicken and vegetarian choices. Alternatively, you might prefer the Duckery Restaurant at Otterton Mill (telephone: 01395 567041). It offers coffees, lunches and cream teas, and although the menu is less wide-ranging than at the King's Arms, it is all home-made and delicious.

---

importance in earlier times.

The walk enables you to explore the delights of the village and enjoy the stunning scenery of the nearby coast, with a beautiful riverside amble between the two. It is all fairly easy walking, and there is the added bonus of the chance to view the birdlife of the Otter estuary.

THE WALK

❶ Head west from Otterton, past Otterton Mill. Notice Mill House opposite the mill, with its Tudor doorway and walled garden. Cross the river Otter, and on the other side of the bridge, turn left through a kissing gate (signposted to Budleigh Salterton). Follow the clear path alongside the river, with a buttercup meadow on your right. After about 500 yards you go through a gate and come to a footbridge across the river on your left. Ignore it and go straight on, and you will eventually pass through another three kissing gates. This is a beautiful and peaceful stretch, with a mass of flowers along the bank in summer and the trees on the other side hanging low over the lazily flowing river; the silence is broken only by the song of the birds.

❷   About 1¹/₂ miles from Otterton, you will come to a road. Turn left, following the Coast Path sign, and cross the bridge. Where the road goes to the left, bear right and make for a gate ahead of you. Go through it and turn right, following the Coast Path sign again. This path takes you along the right-hand side of a field. The river is now on your right, although you can only occasionally see it through the trees. The path takes you down a few steps to cross a wooden footbridge and then up some more steps and to the right of the next field.

About halfway along this field, look out for a bird hide a short distance from the path on the right. From this hide you get a superb view of the estuary and the water-fowl that visit it. Soon after passing the hide, you will be able to see the sea half left.

❸   When you come to a high bank ahead of you, turn left to follow the Coast Path sign. The path climbs fairly gently along the top of the cliff. At the top of the climb, you

---

PLACES of INTEREST

Bicton Park and Pleasure Gardens is only a mile away and offers a variety of entertainment, including beautiful gardens, a woodland railway, an adventure playground and a countryside museum. A little further away (5 miles), on the outskirts of Exmouth, is **A la Ronde**, a 16-sided 18th-century house, now in the hands of the National Trust, which has some fascinating interior decoration.

---

will be rewarded with magnificent views along the coast, views that will remain with you for most of the next 1¹/₂ miles as you skirt the cliffs of this rugged part of the coast. You pass a large pig farm, which seems to go on for miles, and then eventually cross a stile to pass a ruined building. A little further on you will come to a permissive path going left to Otterton. Ignore it and carry straight on along the Coast Path.

❹   About ¹/₂ mile beyond the permissive path there is a stile, beyond which is a public footpath going left, also to Otterton. Take this. It takes you along the left-hand side of a field. At the end of the field is another stile on the left. Cross it and turn immediately right. The path now runs between banks and hedges and comes out at a lane.

❺   When the lane joins a road, turn right and follow the road down a short hill. At the T-junction at the bottom, turn left. At the next T-junction go half left into Otterton.

WIDECOMBE IN THE MOOR

Length : 3³/₄ miles

Getting there: There are several narrow Dartmoor lanes leading to Widecombe, but the easiest route is to turn off the A382 at Bovey Tracey and follow the B3387 past Haytor.	Parking: There is a free car park at one end of the village green and a pay car park at the other.	Maps: OS Landranger 191 Okehampton and North Dartmoor; OS Outdoor Leisure 28 Dartmoor (GR 718768).

W idecombe's fame has spread throughout the world as a result of the old song *Widecombe Fair*, which has been translated into a number of foreign languages, including Japanese! The fair still takes place each year on the second Tuesday in September, when Uncle Tom Cobley rides again, but visitors are drawn to the village throughout the year.

Despite its fame and the crowds of visitors it attracts, Widecombe remains largely unspoilt. It is a lovely village of granite cottages and shops clustered around the village green, with the majestic

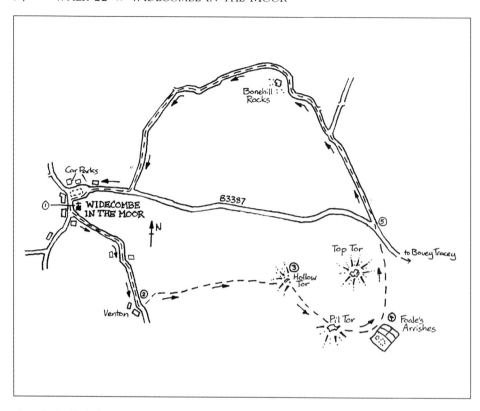

church (called the Cathedral of the Moor because of its spectacular tower) dominating the scene. Notice its roof boss comprising the tin miners' symbol of three rabbits joined in a triangle – evidence of the importance of tin mining in this area in the past. Next to the church is Sexton's Cottages, a 15th-century church house, while the Old Inn, across the road, dates back to the 14th century.

This delightful ramble combines pretty lanes and open moorland, with some superb views. You can explore a few of the tors and rocks around Widecombe and visit the remains of an Iron Age settlement before returning to the village through the beautiful hamlet of Bonehill.

THE WALK

❶ Starting at the church gate, go left and then left again beside Sexton's Cottages, following the signpost to the Rugglestone Inn. The pretty lane takes you down to cross a stream and then winds past a few houses on the right and the Rugglestone Inn on the left. Continue for about ¹⁄₂ mile.

❷ You come to Higher Venton Farm on your right and immediately opposite, you will see a small track leading up the bank. Follow it to the gate that lies straight ahead, ignoring the gates on either side. Go through and follow the track through the gorse, keeping the wall on your left. When it veers off to the left, go straight on along

Pil Tor.

the path, for a long but fairly gentle climb up to Hollow Tor. The path bends to the left below the tor, but you should turn off to climb up towards it; the easiest route is probably to the right of the rocks.

❸ When you get to Hollow Tor, pause to enjoy the view back; it is magnificent, taking in Widecombe, the farms beyond and Hamel Down and the open moor beyond them. Children will also enjoy scrambling among the rocks. Then go on past the tor, bearing slightly right. There are several paths, but it does not matter which you take, as long as you aim for the top of the ridge ahead of you. Soon you will see the rocks of Pil Tor half right; make for

them. Pass to the left of the tor and carry on down to the valley on the other side, aiming for the road ahead.

❹ Soon you will come to the remains of the Foale's Arrishes Iron Age settlement. You cross the ruins of a field boundary and then a number of hut circles, now somewhat overgrown with bracken but still clearly visible. Turn left here and contour round the hill, crossing the remains of more boundary walls as you go.

❺ When you reach the road, follow it to the left until you come to a junction. Turn right here (signposted to Hound Tor, Manaton, Moretonhampstead and Chag-

FOOD and DRINK

Widecombe is well served with places of refreshment. Apart from the village post office and stores, which sells a surprisingly wide variety of provisions, there are two cafés offering teas, coffees and light meals, and two pubs. The Old Inn (telephone: 01364 621207) is right in the centre of the village and is the larger of the two. It offers a wide range of food, including both simple fare, like ploughman's lunches and sausages and chips, and more exotic 'specials' such as garlic prawns, chicken and Brie and lamb in gin sauce. The Rugglestone Inn (telephone: 01364 621327), which is on the edge of the village along the route of this walk, is a much smaller, cosier hostelry with a more restricted menu. There are only about ten main courses available at any one time, but the food, which ranges from ploughman's lunches to home-made pies, is all freshly made and delicious.

ford), and when the main road curves right, take the minor road to the left. This road passes Bonehill Rocks (another excellent place for children to climb and scramble) and then winds steeply down to the valley and back to Widecombe. At the T-junction, turn right to return to your car.

PLACES of INTEREST

Just 2$\frac{1}{2}$ miles from Widecombe is the **Round House Craft Centre** at Buckland in the Moor, with a variety of crafts on view, while 6 miles away, at Bovey Tracey, you will find the **Riverside Centre**, the headquarters of the Devon Guild of Craftsmen. Also at Bovey Tracey are the **Cardew Teapottery**, where you can see teapots being made, and the **House of Marbles**, which has displays of glassblowing. Some 6 miles in the other direction is the **River Dart Country Park**, a children's paradise, while the **Gorse Blossom Miniature Railway and Woodland Park** at Bickington, near Newton Abbot (7$\frac{1}{2}$ miles) offers not only railway rides but also a children's assault course.

BERE FERRERS

Length : 5¹/₂ miles

Getting there: Turn west off the A386 Plymouth to Tavistock road just south of Yelverton and follow the signs to Buckland Monachorum. From there follow the signs to Bere Alston and then Bere Ferrers.

Parking: There is a limited amount of parking at the riverside at the bottom of the village. If that is full, you should be able to park alongside the road in the village.

Map: OS Landranger 201 Plymouth and Launceston (GR 459635).

One of the main attractions of Bere Ferrers is its situation – right on the banks of the river Tavy just above its confluence with the Tamar, and on a promontory bounded by the two rivers. But that is not its only appeal; the whitewashed cottages strung along the lower section of its main street and by the waterside and the fact that it is quite literally the end of the road and therefore unspoilt by passing traffic help to give it its unique charm.

It has a history stretching back to at least

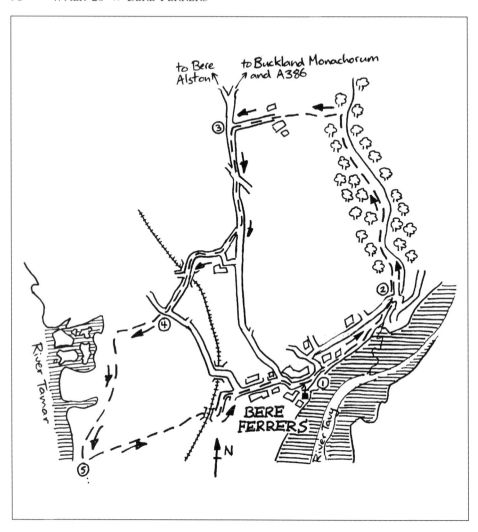

the 13th century, and probably beyond. The church certainly dates back that far, although it was rebuilt in the 14th century. It is of particular interest for its rare French stained glass. The village was a major centre for the mining of silver and lead at that time, although all trace of those industries has long since disappeared and the area is now almost totally agricultural.

The walk takes full advantage of Bere Ferrers' position, giving you two rivers for the price of one. It follows the Tavy upstream before cutting inland through a beautiful stretch of woodland and then crosses the promontory to the floodplains and reed beds of the Tamar, returning to the village across some of the rich farmland that is a feature of this area.

The remains of the village well.

THE WALK

❶ At the riverbank, follow the road round to the left, and at the derestriction sign bear right onto a track that runs alongside the river. It is a lovely stretch of water, with sailing dinghies bobbing with

---

FOOD and DRINK

The village pub is the Old Plough Inn (telephone: 01822 840358), which serves a range of jacket potatoes and other snacks, freshly made main course staples such as steak and kidney pie and lamb hotpot, and a variety of vegetarian dishes. If you prefer to picnic, the small post office and stores stocks a limited but adequate range of ingredients.

---

the tide. The track narrows and you will see a stile and a public footpath sign on your left. Cross it and follow the path through the trees on the other side, still following the river, which you can glimpse through the trees on your right. Cross another stile into a field and keep to the right to reach another stile and gate which take you back onto the path, in front of a row of houses. Go through a gate and follow the path by a hedge to a lane; go straight on.

❷ After a few yards, where the lane turns sharply to the right, go straight on through a gate and into a wood (indicated by a public footpath sign). Continue on the track above a stream. At the fork, take the broader, right-hand track close to the stream. You will soon come to another track leading off to the right; ignore it and carry on with the stream on your right. Ignore the next two tracks, this time on the left, and carry straight on. At the next fork, bear right along the less obvious of the two paths, still keeping to the stream. You cross another stream coming down from the left and shortly afterwards the path takes a sharp turn to the left to climb out of the valley to a stile leading into a field. Go diagonally left across the field to a gate, and immediately beyond it bear right along a path between hedges, marked with a public footpath sign. This leads you to another gate and onto a track. Turn left and follow the track through a farmyard and out onto a lane.

❸   At the T-junction at the end of the lane, turn left. As you follow this new lane down the hill, you get a very good view across farms and woods to the right, and a bit later another lovely panorama opens up down the river ahead of you, with the Tamar Bridge in the middle distance. After about ½ mile, you will see Ley Lane signposted off to the right. Turn right and follow the lane down a hill, crossing a bridge over a railway line, to a T-junction.

❹   Turn right (signposted to Clamoak, Weir Quay and Hole's Hole), and after a few yards go left down a track marked with a public footpath sign. This leads you down to a creek leading off the river Tamar. Go through a gate at the bottom, past a house and straight on to the water's edge. When you get there, turn left, following the yellow waymark, and pass in front of the houses

---

PLACES of INTEREST

The Garden House, near Buckland Monachorum (5½ miles), is a ruined 16th-century vicarage surrounded by 8 acres of beautiful gardens. Just a little further (6 miles) is **Buckland Abbey**, once a Cistercian monastery, then the home of Sir Francis Drake and now run by the National Trust.

---

and into some trees. The path climbs slightly above the water to a gate. Follow the right-hand edge of the field on the other side to another gate. Pick your way across the next field, keeping as close to the water as you can – although you will find it necessary to skirt round to the left to avoid some particularly muddy or overgrown patches. You eventually come to a stile at the other end of the field. Cross it and turn right to go round the edge of the field.

❺   If you would like to go down to the river itself, there is a lovely spot by the water's edge just 200 yards further on where you can picnic. To reach it cross the stile at the end of the field, turn left alongside the floodplain and cross another stile onto the sandy riverbank. Otherwise do not cross the stile but turn left at the fence ahead and follow it up the hill. As you do so, you get some superb views behind you. At the top of the field, you go through a gate. Keep to the right of the next field to another gate and go straight across a third field to a stile which leads to a track. Bear right beyond the stile and follow the track under a railway line to join a lane. Where the lane meets Station Road go straight on, and at the T-junction go right to return to the bottom of the village.

MEAVY

Length : 3 miles

Getting there: There are various routes to Meavy, all along narrow lanes, but the best approach is to turn south off the B3212 Yelverton to Princetown road at Dousland and follow the signs to the village.

Parking: You can park either round the village green or in the car park behind the parish hall.

Maps: OS Landranger 201 Plymouth and Launceston (start and finish) and 202 Torbay and South Dartmoor (middle section); OS Outdoor Leisure 28 Dartmoor (GR 540672).

This is an old village – it is mentioned in the Domesday Book, but it is believed that the original church was built in the time of King Knut (Canute), in the early 11th century. The present church, however, is Norman, and was substantially rebuilt in the 13th and 15th centuries. It also seems to have been quite an important centre, with its own mill, which was owned by the descendants of Sir Francis Drake (the old mill house, at the west of the village, is now a listed building). The old monastic route

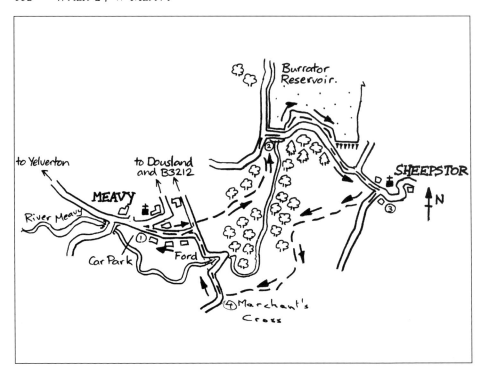

from Plympton Priory to Tavistock Abbey crossed the river Meavy just to the east of the village, and Marchant's Cross, one of the crosses which marked the route, can still be seen. It dates back to at least the 13th century, and it is said that travellers about to set off across Dartmoor knelt here and prayed for a safe journey.

The focal point of the village is the green, with the pub, the Royal Oak, alongside and the church tucked in behind

---

FOOD and DRINK

The fare at the Royal Oak (telephone: 01822 852944) ranges from sandwiches and pasties to substantial main courses such as steak and kidney pie and a range of fish and vegetarian dishes.

---

it. At one end of the green is the Meavy Oak, a massive tree which is said to be at least 500 years old and is now supported by props. Tradition has it that itinerant clerics used to preach here and the tree (or its predecessor – the Meavy Oak is mentioned in the Domesday Book) was planted to shelter their 'congregation'.

Not far from Meavy is Burrator Reservoir, a lovely, peaceful spot. On this walk we visit it, as well as the delightful little hamlet of Sheepstor, which despite its much-reduced size now was once an important centre for the wool trade. The route is mainly through woodland, with a few farm tracks and country lanes in between, and on the way back to Meavy it follows a short stretch of the old monastic route, passing Marchant's Cross.

The old vicarage at Sheepstor.

THE WALK

❶ Turn right from the car park and head east out of the village. Pass a school on your right and at the road junction follow the main road round to the left (signposted to Dousland). After a few yards you will see a public footpath sign on the right, pointing to Burrator Dam. Go through a gate and across the field on the other side to a track in amongst some trees. This goes through two gates and into a wood. Soon after the second gate, bear left up a path, marked with a yellow dot painted on a tree. You will find similar dots painted on trees and rocks at regular intervals through the wood to indicate the path. You come to a fork; go left up a broad track, again following the yellow waymarks. You climb to a bank and bear right to follow it round. Cross a wall and follow the path alongside a dry leat to a track; bear left, again following the yellow waymarks, and go up the track to a road. Turn right and follow the road to Burrator Reservoir.

❷ At the dam wall, turn right (signposted to Sheepstor) to follow the road across the wall. You get a lovely view over the reservoir on your left, with Leather Tor at the far end. At the end of the wall the lane goes round to the left. Just before it winds to the right you will see a stile on your left. Cross it to go down to the bank of the reservoir and turn right along the beautiful rhododendron-fringed path at the bottom. This runs alongside the lane, but it makes much more pleasant walking. Ignore the next stile leading back to the lane and follow the path until it emerges from the trees by a second dam wall. Cross the stile you will see on your right here to rejoin the lane and turn left. The lane meanders along, with the great bulk of Sheeps Tor looming over it, and then swings right into the pretty little hamlet of the same name.

❸   At the cross in the centre of Sheepstor, turn right down another lane. It crosses a stream and swings to the left; just after it does so, turn right down a track (signposted to Marchant's Cross). Follow the track round to the left into a field. Cross the field to a gateway in the far corner, and almost immediately beyond it turn left through a gate into another field. Turn right and follow the right-hand edge of the field to a stone stile. Follow the path beyond round to the right of the next field to another stile and then go right into a wood. Bear left and make your way through the wood, following the yellow waymarks which once again indicate the path.

At the end of the wood go left up a wall and then drop down via a ladder to a sunken track going right. It soon joins a more well-defined track; as you follow this, you get a very good view on your right, across the wood to Meavy and the farms beyond. The track swings to the right

PLACES of INTEREST

The **Yelverton Paperweight Centre**, just under 2 miles away, has an unusual display of over 800 glass paperweights. **The Garden House** at Buckland Monachorum (3 miles) has superb gardens, and just down the road from there is the National Trust property of **Buckland Abbey**, once the home of Sir Francis Drake. And at Princetown, about 5 miles away, the Dartmoor National Park Authority's **High Moorland Visitor Centre** is well worth a visit for its displays and presentations on the history and life of Dartmoor.

across a cattle grid; just before it does so bear left across a stile, following the path sign. Go down alongside a field to another stile and then a third which takes you into another wood. Follow the path down to a dry stream bed and go right. Cross the stream bed at the bottom and keep to the right of the field on the other side to a gate. This brings you out onto a track which almost immediately becomes a surfaced road.

❹   At the T-junction at the end is Marchant's Cross. Turn right here and follow the road down, across a cattle grid, to the river. The road takes a sharp bend to the right to cross the river via a bridge, but you can cut straight down and cross it via the stepping stones that were used by the monks of old. Rejoin the road on the other side and at the junction turn left (signposted to Yelverton) to return to Meavy.

STOKEINTEIGNHEAD

Length : 4½ miles

Getting there: Stokeinteignhead is about a mile west of the B3199 Teignmouth to Torquay road and a similar distance south of the Newton Abbot to Shaldon road, and is	signposted from both directions. **Parking:** You should be able to find somewhere to park in the road through the village.	**Maps:** OS Landranger 202 Torbay and South Dartmoor; OS Explorer 31 Torquay and Dawlish (GR 916705).

You may wonder at the name of this village (which, incidentally, is pronounced 'Stoke-in-teen-head'), since the head-waters of the Teign are many miles away on Dartmoor. In fact it has been corrupted over the centuries; it was originally 'ten

hides', not 'Teignhead', a hide being a unit of land area.

The village nestles in the valley of the Arch Brook, a picturesque collection of traditional whitewashed cottages, some thatched and some slate-roofed. The

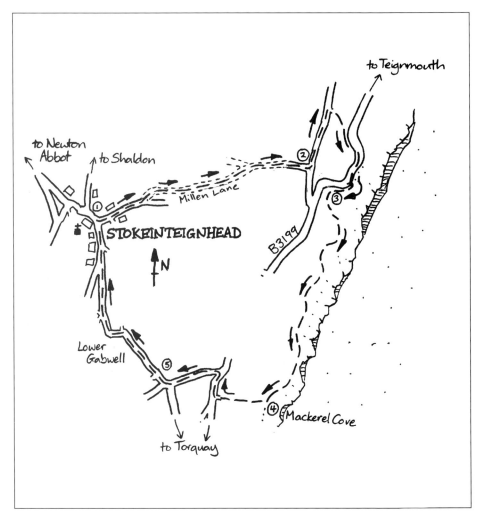

attractive church, which boasts an interesting 14th-century screen, is set slightly above the road through the village, with its companion the Church House Inn (which, as its name suggests, was originally built to house visitors to and workers on the church) below it.

The coast is not far away, and this particular stretch is magnificent, with its rugged cliffs and isolated coves. The walk takes farm tracks to the cliff-top and then follows the South Devon Coast Path for about 1½ miles before returning along pretty country lanes. The views are quite outstanding, not only along the coast, but also across the Teign estuary and the rich, rolling South Devon farmland. They come at a price, however, and there are a few stiff climbs, especially along the Coast Path.

A view from the South Devon Coast Path.

FOOD and DRINK

There are two establishments I can particularly recommend in Stokeinteignhead. The Church House Inn in the centre of the village (telephone: 01626 872475) is a pretty thatched pub, full of atmosphere, whose menu ranges from bar snacks to fresh fish, steaks and vegetarian dishes. The Chaser's Arms (telephone: 01626 873670) is a lovely restaurant to the south of the village. It offers a range of bar snacks, fish dishes and casseroles, but being a restaurant it cannot serve drinks without food. Teas, coffees and light meals are also available from the Old Bakery Tea Room, opposite the Church House Inn.

THE WALK

❶ Take the road immediately opposite the Church House Inn (signposted to Teignmouth) and follow it out of the village. At the village sign, where the lane bends to the right, go left up another lane, which is marked with a 'no through road' sign. This soon deteriorates into an unsurfaced track. It goes to the right past some farm buildings and begins to climb, gently at first but more steeply as you go along. You get a very good view back across the village and the rich farmland that surrounds it. At the top of the hill you join another track, where you get another lovely view across the Teign estuary to Bishopsteignton and Teignmouth. Turn right onto the new track, which continues to climb, but more gently. Towards the end you get a lovely view to the right along the coast.

❷   It eventually comes out at a lane; turn left. As you go down the hill, the whole of Teignmouth seafront is laid out before you. After about 400 yards you will find a public footpath sign pointing across a stile on the right. Follow it down towards the sea and then to the right to cross two more stiles. You end up in a rather overgrown area alongside the main Teignmouth to Torquay road, then go through a gate and onto the road itself. Turn right and follow the road for about 100 yards or so. Do take care, however, as it is a busy stretch. Just after a right-hand bend you will find a Coast Path sign pointing half left off the road. Go down the path, which runs just below the road for a short distance and then climbs up to rejoin it, this time along a pavement. Go round the next right-hand bend, and the pavement ends at another Coast Path sign.

❸   Turn left and follow the path down some steps. It twists to the right and then to the left, and then goes steeply down between fences to the cliff-top, where it bears right to follow the line of the cliffs. After a while, it turns right and you climb steeply up some steps. Pause at the top to get your breath back and to enjoy the magnificent view back along the coast, all the way into Dorset. As you follow the path, you get another good view around Torbay ahead of you.

The path descends again and you enter a copse. After a while it climbs to the right again up some steps, and at the top you get

---

PLACES of INTEREST

At Shaldon, about 1³/₄ miles away, is the **Shaldon Wildlife Trust**, a small zoo which specialises in rare and endangered species. The major holiday centre of Torquay (3¹/₂ miles) has a wide range of attractions, including boat trips, the **Babbacombe Model Village**, the cave system at **Kents Cavern** and **Bygones**, a reconstruction of a Victorian street. And **Tucker's Maltings**, 4¹/₂ miles away in Newton Abbot, offers guided tours of a working malthouse.

---

another good view around Torbay. It descends again and at the bottom the lovely stretch back along the coast comes into view again. There are not many more climbs to negotiate, and those that there are are quite gentle in comparison to what has gone before. A few hundred yards after leaving the copse you will see a path on the right across a V-stile. Ignore it and continue along a relatively level stretch of path. After about 700 yards the path turns to the right and climbs slightly.

❹   As it goes to the left again, just beyond a bench, turn right up another path (signposted to the main road and Higher Gabwell). The path leads to a track; bear left and you will come out onto the main road. Turn right, follow the road carefully for about 150 yards and then turn left into Gabwell Hill. This takes you down into the valley to a crossroads.

❺   Turn right here into an attractive lane, full of interest, which leads you through the pretty hamlet of Lower Gabwell back to Stokeinteignhead.

TUCKENHAY

Length : 3³/4 miles

Getting there: Tuckenhay lies down narrow country lanes about 3 miles south-east of Totnes and about 6 miles north-west of Dartmouth. It can be approached from the north by turning off the A381 Totnes to Kingsbridge road just outside Totnes and following the signs, from the west by turning off the same road at Harbertonford and again following the signs, and from the south, via Cornworthy, by turning off the A3122 Totnes to Dartmouth road.

Parking: The only parking is along the road. This is not very wide in Tuckenhay itself, so you may need to go to the edge of the village to find space. Please park with consideration for others.

Maps: OS Landranger 202 Torbay and South Dartmoor; OS Outdoor Leisure 20 South Devon (GR 818562).

Situated right on Bow Creek, where the rivers Harbourne and Wash empty into the river Dart, Tuckenhay is a picturesque little village in a delightful situation. It consists of a collection of stone and slate or cob and thatch houses and cottages in a string

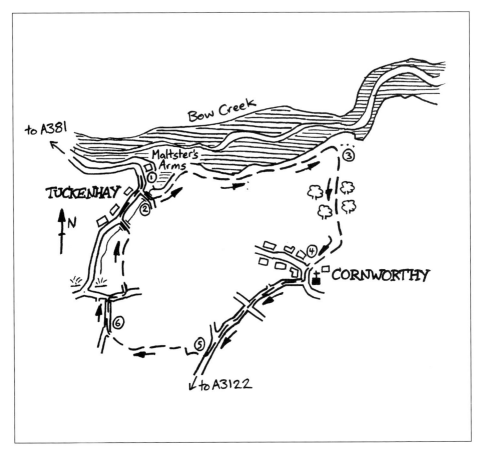

along the lane and the creek. On the outskirts, just up the valley of the Wash, is a lovely old paper mill which dates back to 1829 and is now used as a private holiday centre, and lower down, on the creek itself,

---

FOOD and DRINK

The village pub, the Maltster's Arms (telephone: 01803 732350), has an excellent menu, which ranges from snacks and sandwiches through light meals such as pork and herb sausages and chicken stir-fry to mouthwatering offerings like game pie and huntsman's casserole.

---

is an old cider press.

The village pub, the Maltster's Arms, is full of character and very much in keeping with the rest of the village. It was owned for some time by TV chef Keith Floyd, who changed the name to Floyd's Inn and put up a sign which read 'Floyd's Inn (sometimes)'! It has now been sold again, and has reverted to its original name.

Just up the road is the rather larger Domesday village of Cornworthy, with its 15th-century church to the east and the gatehouse of a medieval Augustinian priory – all that remains of the original building –

The village of Cornworthy visited on the walk.

to the west. This walk takes you along the bank of Bow Creek, which is usually full of wildfowl, to Cornworthy, then returns to Tuckenhay via farm paths and quiet lanes which show you the farmland and woodland of this area at their best.

THE WALK

❶ Because there is no central parking area, I will start the directions for the walk at the Maltster's Arms, as that is the nearest Tuckenhay has to a central point. Go east from there (ie left as you come out of the door) and follow the road round to the right.

❷ You come to a bridge across the river

Wash on your left. Cross over and immediately on the other side turn left across a stile, following the public footpath sign. This takes you down along the riverbank and into a small copse. You go through a kissing gate into a field, and soon the path goes round to the right, following the bank of Bow Creek. The path widens to a track and climbs some way above the creek. Soon, however, you will see a narrower path going off to the left down towards the creek, indicated by a yellow waymark. Follow this path down. At the junction, go to the left to cross a stile to a meadow alongside the water. The path then goes slightly away from the creek up some steps and along to a stile into a wood.

❸   You cross another stile into a field with a couple of isolated oak trees. Go right in this field and follow the left-hand hedge up to a track. At the top, follow the track round to the right and through a farmyard and you will come out at Cornworthy parish hall, just in front of the church.

❹   Turn left and keep following the main road round to the right (signposted to Tideford and Dartmouth). The lane climbs rather steeply and steadily between hedges until you come to a crossroads. Go straight on (signposted to Tideford and Dartmouth again). You get a very good view over to your right and behind you as you do so, across the rich, undulating farmland of the South Hams. You pass a lane going off to the right, and about 100 yards further on you will see a public footpath sign in a hedge, pointing down a track on the right.

❺   Turn off here and when the track goes up to a house bear right along a narrow path down some steps to a stile. Cross the stile and keep to the left of the field on the other side. When the hedge takes a turn to the left, go straight on for a few more yards to a post with a yellow waymark on. Turn left here and follow a path across the middle of the field to a stile followed by two footbridges and another stile. After the second stile turn right and keep to the right of the field. At the bottom follow the hedge

---

PLACES of INTEREST

Bowden House, 2 miles towards Totnes, is a lovely 13th-century house and photographic museum. **Totnes** itself is a very attractive walled town with a castle, a motor museum and an Elizabethan museum. It is also one of the termini for the **South Devon Railway**, a steam railway which plies between Buckfastleigh and Totnes along the lovely Dart valley. In the opposite direction, the **Woodland Leisure Park** (4 miles) offers a wide range of exciting rides and slides. The historic port of **Dartmouth** (6 miles) is also worth a visit, not only for its beautiful architecture and narrow streets, but also for its interesting museum and castle, and for the boat trips that are on offer, up the river Dart and along the coast.

---

round to the left until you come to a gate. This leads onto a track past some farm buildings and to a gate onto a lane.

❻   Turn right and after about 200 yards you come to a T-junction. Turn right again, and after about 100 yards you will find a house called Edgecombe Barn on your left. Turn left here, past the house, onto a track. This leads you between a combination of hedges, fences and walls through some woodland and out onto a lane. Bear right and you will pass the old mill on your left. Follow the lane round to the left across the river Wash and at the T-junction at the main road turn right to return to Tuckenhay.

WALK 27

NOSS MAYO

Length : 4 miles

Getting there: Turn south off the A379 Plymouth to Kingsbridge road onto the B3186 at Yealmpton and follow the signs to Noss Mayo.

Parking: There is a free public car park near the

southern edge of the village, but it is not signposted. To reach it, turn right down Revelstoke Road just past the church as you enter the village. At the crossroads, where Revelstoke Road takes a sharp turn to the right down to the water, go

straight on and the car park is on the left next to some tennis courts.

Maps: OS Landranger 201 Plymouth and Launceston; OS Outdoor Leisure 20 South Devon (GR 547474).

Noss Mayo ('Matthew's headland') is a picturesque village which clings to the hillside above Newton Creek near the mouth of the river Yealm. It contains a good mixture of architectural styles, with the older cottages clustered around the water's edge and more modern housing climbing up the side of the valley.

It was once a fishing community, and the 16th-century Old Ship Inn on the water-

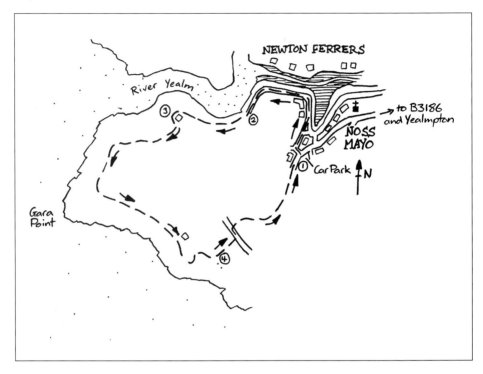

front was a popular haunt of smugglers. Its main activity today, however, is sailing. Together with its larger counterpart Newton Ferrers on the other side of the creek, it is a popular yachting centre, as you can see from the number of boats moored in the creek and pulled up onto the slipway in the centre of the village.

The headland which gives the village its name was once part of Lord Revelstoke's estate, and much of this walk follows the route of a carriage drive which he constructed at the end of the 19th century. It runs alongside Newton Creek, mainly through beautiful woodland, to the river Yealm and then swings round the headland to follow the coast before returning along farm tracks to Noss Mayo. There are some truly magnificent coastal views and hardly

any effort is needed to enjoy them – there is very little climbing, and what there is can only be described as gentle.

THE WALK

❶   Cross the road from the car park and follow the lane on the other side as it bends to the right. When it bends to the right again to join the main road, go straight on along a path in front of some cottages. When the path joins the road a little further on, bear left and follow the road as it curves left alongside the creek and into a wood, with the cottages of Noss Mayo's twin village of Newton Ferrers across the water.

❷   At the gateway at the end of the road bear right onto a track following the Coast

The Yealm estuary.

Path sign to Stoke. At the end of the track, bear right onto a path, following the Coast Path sign again. It takes you between hedges and past Ferryman's Cottage into a

FOOD and DRINK

The Old Ship Inn on the western side of the inlet which almost divides the village in two is very pleasant (telephone: 01752 872387). Its age, its history and its situation – set into the hillside right on the waterfront – makes it most appealing. It also has a wide-ranging and delicious menu, from pasties and snacks to a variety of fish dishes and traditional favourites such as steak and kidney pie. There is also a post office and stores in the village for those who want to make up a picnic.

wood. This is a lovely stretch, with the wood climbing up the hill on your left and the river Yealm just visible through the trees on your right. After a while the path climbs to join a track; bear right and follow the track through a gate and past a group of houses.

❸   At the junction, ignore the path that goes off to the right and keep following the track as it bends sharply to the left to more open ground. You pass some more cottages and then go through another gate and continue along the track on the other side as it takes a bend to the right. Look back from here for a superb view along the coast, with the Great Mew Stone in the fore-

PLACES of INTEREST

Kitley Caves, 3 miles away, are well worth a visit, not only for the caves themselves but also for the Stone Age museum which is part of the same complex. A bit further afield (4 miles) is the **National Shire Horse Centre** outside Yealmpton, where you can get close to these majestic animals and see them at work. And of course Plymouth, just 9 miles away, offers a wealth of attractions, including the historic Hoe and Barbican and the **Plymouth Dome**, a superb exhibition and discovery centre where among other things you can experience life in the city in Elizabethan times and during the Blitz.

ground. You enter another wood and then, after about 600 yards, cross a stile to more open ground. From here you get another stunning view across the Yealm estuary and Wembury Bay. You may hear the guns firing from HMS Cambridge across the bay. The track rounds Gara Point, and soon afterwards you come to a gate and then another one with a stile alongside. The track leads you to Warren Cottage, where two more gates await you, and then curves to the right around the headland of Blackstone Point. You get another superb view along the coast to the right from here.

❹   Once round the headland, the track turns inland slightly and you come to a gate and a stile. Go through and follow the track on the other side away from the coast. Another stile takes you into a lane; turn left and after a few yards right down another track (signposted to Noss Mayo). When you come to a farm, follow the track round to the right of the farmhouse and down the valley. It leads to a surfaced lane, which in turn runs down to Noss Mayo, and the car park is on your right.

WALK 28
RINGMORE
Length : 3¹/₂ miles

Getting there: Take the B3392 south off the A379 Plymouth to Kingsbridge road just east of Modbury, turn right at St Ann's Chapel and follow the signs to Ringmore.

Parking: The only public parking is on the road, and since the lanes in the lower part of the village are rather narrow, I would suggest that you park in the upper road which skirts round to the east (there are two marked parking places by the phone box near the end of the village). If you are patronising the Journey's End, the landlord may allow you to leave your car in the pub car park at the entrance to the village while you walk – but do ask first.

Maps: OS Landranger 202 Torbay and South Dartmoor; OS Outdoor Leisure 20 South Devon (GR 652460).

The manor of Reimora appears in the Domesday Book, so the village has quite a long pedigree. Its association with smuggling over the centuries is revealed in names such as Smuggler's Cottage and Smugglers' Lane. During the Civil War, a party of parliamentary troops landed at nearby Ayrmer Cove in order to capture

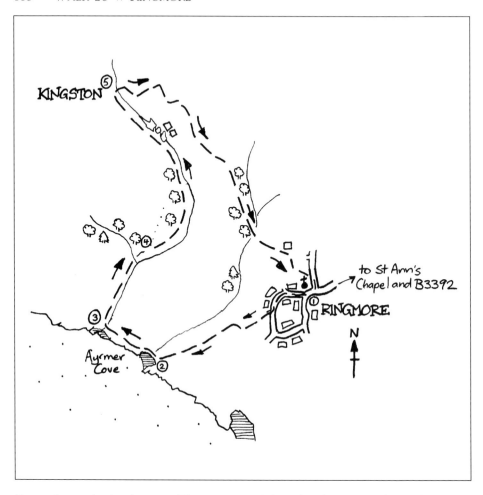

Parson Lane, the local rector. They managed to destroy the rectory, but Lane hid in
the church tower for three months before
escaping to France.

FOOD and DRINK

The Journey's End (telephone: 01548 810205)
offers a wide range of fare, from sandwiches
and snacks to a mouthwatering array of main
courses, and the post office and stores sells
provisions.

The church is mainly 14th-century,
although parts of it are even older, and it
stands on the very edge of the village at the
top of the hill. The village itself consists of
steep lanes lined with beautifully kept cob
and thatch cottages, most dating from the
16th-18th centuries. The pub, which is
near the bottom of the village, is a 13th-
century building which was licensed as an
ale house at the time of Elizabeth I. It was
called the New Inn, but changed its name
to the Journey's End soon after the First

World War – *Journey's End* was the title of a play by R. C. Sherriff, part of which he is said to have written while staying there.

THE WALK

❶ Starting from the church, turn right outside the gate and follow the lane down, past the pub and steeply up to the left beyond it. Near the top, turn right down another lane past a house called Smuggler's Cottage. At the end, at a gate into a private garden, bear left, following the public bridlepath sign. The broad path runs between hedges to a gate, and then on between hedges on the other side. It is a lovely path, ideal for blackberrying in the late summer and autumn. About 1/2 mile after leaving Ringmore the hedge opens out and you get an impressive view of the cliffs ahead of you. A little further on you reach the coast at Ayrmer Cove.

❷ Turn right here, cross a small footbridge and climb to the top of the cliff beyond. It is a steep but mercifully short climb, and when you reach the top you get a very good view back along the coast, with Burgh Island in the middle distance. The path rounds the headland, and as it does so the panorama back along the coast becomes even more stunning. You also begin to get a good view along the coast ahead of you. After a while you go down a steep hill to another cove called Westcombe Beach.

❸ Cross a footbridge, and on the other side turn sharp right, following the permissive footpath sign to Kingston. The path runs between a fence and a stream for about 500 yards, and then turns right to cross a footbridge. A short distance beyond

the footbridge you come to a stile, and immediately on the other side the path forks.

❹ Take the path which goes straight on (signposted to Kingston), and it will take you a little way to the left of the stream and in among some trees to a beautiful stretch of woodland. After about 1/2 mile you pass a reservoir and then a string of broad pools. The path joins a track; bear right and it will soon join another, more well-defined track coming in from the water treatment works on the right. Go straight on here and follow the track until it joins a lane on the edge of the village of Kingston.

❺ Turn right as soon as you reach the lane, following the public footpath sign to Ringmore. Cross a stile and go across a field to a gate, then across an area that has been newly planted with trees to a stile. Keep to the left of the field on the other side, and turn right at the end just before a gap in the hedge, to follow the edge of the field round. The view ahead and to the right here is very good. At the end of the field cross a stile, and then another stile into a lane. Turn left and after a few yards go right across yet another stile (signposted to Ringmore). Cross a field, with pleasant views all around you, and then cross another stile to a track. Turn left and follow the track round to the right. When you come to a gap in the hedge on your left, marked with a yellow arrow, go through it and down the left-hand side of the field. At the bottom turn right, and after about 100 yards or so bear left down a broad track into a wood.

PLACES of INTEREST

The **Sorley Tunnel Adventure Farm**, 6 miles away outside Kingsbridge, is an organic farm with craft workshops and an adventure play area attached. Some 9 miles in the other direction, near Yealmpton, is the **National Shire Horse Centre**, where you can see these beautiful animals at work.

At the bottom, where the track swings left to ford a stream, go straight on, keeping the stream on your left. Cross a stile and continue alongside the stream. At the end of the next field, cross the stream, go through a gate and follow the path on the other side into a copse. As you leave the copse you come to a junction in the path; go right, following the yellow waymark, and climb steeply up a field to a stile. Turn left on the other side, and after a few yards right throughout a gateway. Keep to the left and you will find a gate on your left, halfway down the field. Go through it and diagonally right across the next field to another gate into another field. Keep left to reach a kissing gate, which leads you out into a lane. Turn right to return to the church.

LODDISWELL

Length : 4¹/₂ miles

Getting there: The village is about 3 miles north of Kingsbridge, and is signposted off the A381 Kingsbridge bypass. If you are approaching from the north, turn south off the A38 at Wrangaton Cross, just south-west of South Brent, follow the A3121 to Kitterford Cross and turn left, following the signs to Loddiswell.

Parking: There is a free public car park just off the main road through the village.

Maps: OS Landranger 202 Torbay and South Dartmoor; OS Outdoor Leisure 20 South Devon (GR 720486).

Loddiswell's network of little lanes makes it a fascinating place to explore – one never knows what one will find around the next corner. There is an interesting mixture of architectural styles, from traditional white-washed cob and unrendered stone to Victorian and modern brick rendering.

It is somewhat unusual in that, far from being the focal point of the village, the attractive 14th-century church is on the very edge, and easily missed if one is just passing through. The village centre, if it

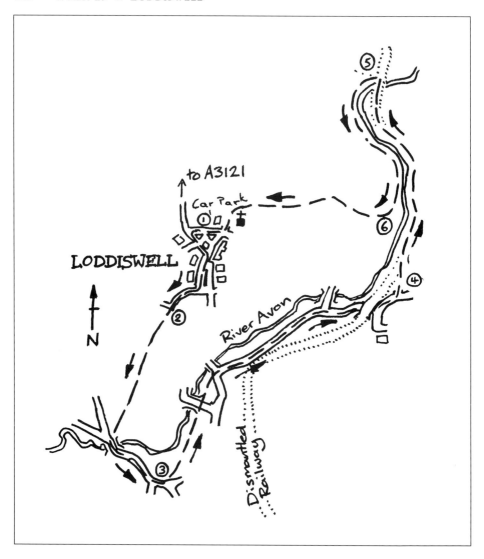

can be said to have one, is dominated by the pub, with the post office and the shop set back in different directions.

The river Avon passes just to the east of Loddiswell, and it will be your companion for much of the walk. The route takes farm paths and tracks to the river, and then follows it upstream across fields and

through the stunningly beautiful Wood-
leigh Wood before returning to the village
via paths and lanes.

THE WALK

❶ Leave the car park via the vehicle exit
and turn right. At the T-junction turn left.
Where the main road turns sharp left, go
straight on, down Fore Street. When that
goes sharp left, turn right along Town's
Lane, which takes you out of the village.

❷ On the outskirts of the village, it turns
sharp right. As it does so, go straight on
across a stile marked with a public footpath
sign. Follow the left-hand edge of a field to
a gap in the hedge ahead, and then keep to
the left of the next field to a stile. You get a
very good view all around you. Keep to the
left of the next field to another stile, and
then go straight across the next to a gateway.
Keep to the right of the next field to a gate
on the right; go through and bear left across
another field to a stone stile, which leads
you onto a narrow track between banks.
Turn left and follow the track to a lane,
then turn left again. The lane follows the
gently flowing river Avon before turning
away from it. It curves to the left and you
pass a junction, with a road going off to the
right.

❸ After a few yards, just before the next
junction, turn left across a stile marked with
a public footpath sign and a yellow waymark. Follow the line of the stream on your
left and as it veers to the left, bear half left
to cross a footbridge. Go straight on to
rejoin the river Avon and follow it upstream
to a stile. Keep to the left of the next field,
with the river still on your left, but now

behind a screen of trees. At the end of this
field is a bridge, with some steps going up to
the right of it to a road. Cross the road and
go down some more steps on the other side.
Keep to the left of another field, still
following the river, and cross a stone stile at
the end into a lane. Bear left, but do not
turn immediately left to cross the river;
instead, follow the main lane, keeping the
river on your left, but now a short distance
away. After about $^1/_2$ mile you come to a
road going off to your left, and a few
hundred yards beyond that the lane goes to
the right under a disused railway line, then
to the left again.

❹ When it takes another turn to the
right, you will find the old Loddiswell
station, now a private house, on your left.
Cross a stile just beyond it onto a path
which runs between a fence on the left and
an embankment on the right. You enter a
very pretty wood, and after a few yards you
come to a stile on your left. You now have a
choice: you can either follow the public
footpath to the right of the fence or cross
the stile and follow a permissive path to the
left of it. There is not a great deal to choose
between the two – they run more or less
parallel to each other through a lovely wood
– but my preference is for the permissive
path, if only because it is closer to the river.
It has the added attraction of following the
track of the old railway, which was called
the Primrose Line for reasons which are
beautifully apparent if you follow it in the
early spring. After about $^3/_4$ mile, you cross
the river via the old railway bridge.
Immediately on the other side, go down
some steps on the left and follow the
opposite bank downstream.

❺ After a few yards you will come to a fork in the path; go left alongside the river, cross a footbridge and then a stile into a field. Keep to the left along the bank to another stile, which takes you back into the wood. After a while you will find that you have to negotiate a few fallen trees, but they do not present too much of a problem. The path leaves the bank for a short distance, and then goes left across a footbridge to rejoin it and continues downstream. After a while you will have to duck under another fallen tree and then cross a stile on your right. Turn immediately left again and the path takes you out of the wood and across a field.

❻ At the end of the field, go right alongside a tributary stream, following the public footpath sign. After a short distance go left to cross the stream and bear right. You have to negotiate yet another fallen tree, and then follow the path upstream; soon you will find a bank on your left, and

---

PLACES of INTEREST

A mile south of Loddiswell is the **Sorley Tunnel Adventure Farm**, which incorporates a working organic farm, an adventure playground and craft workshops. About 1¹/₂ miles to the north are **Loddiswell Rings**, an Iron Age hill-fort, on which the Normans built a motte and bailey castle. Also worth a visit is the **Stancombe Cyder Press** (4 miles) near Sherford, which offers a tour of the cider works.

---

the path runs between it and the stream. After a while you cross a stile on your left and then bear right to continue upstream. You pass a farm on your right and then go through a gate into a lane. Go straight on, with an attractive view to your right as you go, and the lane leads you back to Loddiswell, bringing you out alongside the church. Follow the road round to the left, and immediately beyond the post office turn right and then right again to return to the car park.

SLAPTON

Length : 6³/₄ miles

Getting there: Turn north-west off the A379 Dartmouth to Kingsbridge road 1¹/₂ miles north of Torcross. Alternatively you can turn off the A381 Totnes to Kingsbridge road just south of Halwell and follow the narrow lanes across country.

Parking: There are a few places where you can park along the road in Slapton itself, or you can use the pull-in on the edge of the village towards the beach. As a last resort, you could park in the beach car park and start the walk there.

Maps: OS Landranger 202 Torbay and South Dartmoor; OS Outdoor Leisure 20 South Devon (GR 821450).

Slapton is a particularly beautiful example of a traditional South Devon village, with its variety of old stone and cob and thatch cottages and its narrow, winding streets. From a distance, the feature that seems to dominate the village is the tower of a 14th-century chantry, now ruined, below which is tucked the Tower Inn. The church is also 14th century, and although it looks almost insignificant by comparison, it is very attractive.

Slapton Ley, which lies just outside the

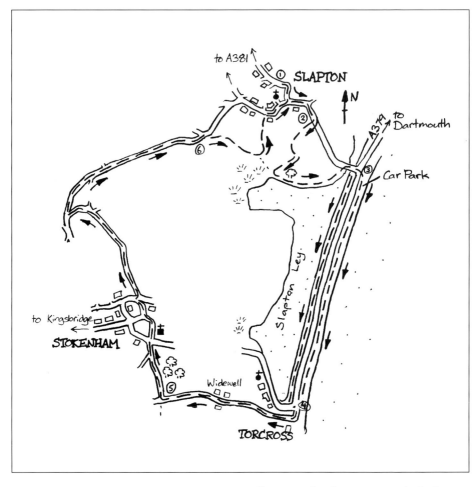

village, is the largest natural freshwater body in south-west England. It is a nature reserve and a Site of Special Scientific Interest, and is an important stopping-off place for migrating birds, as well as a breeding ground for a number of species. Slapton Sands, just across the sand bank from the ley, is a magnificent beach, stretching for 3 miles from Torcross in the south to Strete in the north. This lovely walk visits both the ley and the sands, as well as the villages of Torcross and

Slapton Lea and Sands seen from the village of Torcross.

Stokenham, along easy paths and quiet country lanes.

THE WALK

❶ The best place to start the walk if you have managed to park in the village itself is the church. The route also passes both the pull-in on the outskirts and the beach car park, so if you have parked in either of these places you may prefer to start there and visit the village on your way back.

From the main gate to the church then, turn east (right as you come out of the gate). Follow the road round to the right, and then go left (signposted to the beach).

❷ Pass the Slapton Ley Field Studies Centre on your left, and about 100 yards beyond it turn right down the drive of South Grounds Farm. At the bend in the drive, you will find a stile on your right; cross it and turn left, following the public footpath sign. The path takes you down a field and into a wood. There is a right-hand bend and the path goes down towards Slapton Ley. Cross a stile at the end and go straight on (signposted to Slapton Sands via the nature trail). At the bottom the path goes down to the left to skirt round the ley. If you look to your right as you follow it, you may see some of the waterfowl that make it their home. You cross a number of stiles and go up and down steps as you follow the path round the ley, and eventually you come out, through a gate, onto a road. Turn right and follow the road across a bridge.

❸ On the other side of the bridge you have a choice of paths. The route follows the line of the main road for some 1½ miles to Torcross, but you can choose whether you go to the right of the road, alongside the ley, or to the left, along the beach. If you want to go alongside the ley, turn right along a path before you reach the main road; if you want to follow the beach, cross the road and then turn right. Both have their attractions – the ley route is filled with wild flowers for much of the year and the beach route gives you a lovely view along this long stretch of sand.

If you follow the path, you will come out at a car park on the edge of Torcross, and you will find a hide on your right where you can sit and watch the birdlife on the ley. From the car park you should cross the road and continue along the left-hand side.

If you go along the beach, you will come out on the promenade at Torcross. You should follow it to the end and then turn right towards the main road.

❹ Where the main road turns right (and just where you join it if you have come along the promenade), there is a small lane going straight on up a hill, to the right of the Village Inn. Follow it up and round to the right, and you will get a superb view across Torcross to the ley and Slapton Sands, and all the way back along the coast. The lane continues to climb, passing through the hamlet of Widewell.

❺ About ¼ mile beyond Widewell you

PLACES of INTEREST

Stancombe Cyder Press, 5 miles away, off the road from Slapton to the A381, offers tours of the centre, while the **Woodland Leisure Park** (5 miles north of Slapton) is the place to go for exciting rides, slides and other children's attractions. **Dartmouth**, 6 miles away, is a picturesque port, steeped in maritime history, where you can take boat trips up the river Dart and out to sea or visit the museum and castle.

---

will find a lane leading off to the right towards a wood. Turn down it and follow it through the wood at the bottom of the hill. It emerges at a main road at Stokenham. Cross the road to follow the lane that runs up between the church and the Church House Inn. Just before you get to the Sportsman's Arms, turn right up another small lane. It climbs steeply up to a T-junction, where you turn right and immediately left again. The lane continues to climb for some distance and then descends quite steeply. It bends to the left past Frittiscombe Farm and just beyond the farm you come to another T-junction. Turn right and follow another lane for a little under a mile to a bridge.

❻ Just beyond the bridge is a path to the right, signposted to Marsh Lane. Turn down it and follow it through a wood, alongside a stream. On the other side of the wood it emerges at a bed of rushes and you will soon come to a path junction. Go straight on (signposted to Slapton village) to a stile leading to a track. Follow the track up the left-hand side of a field and through a gate at the end. The track finally comes out at a T-junction, where you should turn right to return to the village.